4·50

GW00634513

PHOTOTYPOGRAPHY
a guide to in-house typesetting & design

Charles Scribner's Sons
New York

PHOTO TYPOGRAPHY

by allan haley

a guide to in-house typesetting & design

Copyright © 1980 Allan Haley

Library of Congress Cataloging in Publication Data

Haley, Allan.
    Phototypography: a guide to in-house
typesetting and design

    Includes index.
    1. Phototypesetting. I. Title.
TR1010.H34   686.2'25   79-20403
ISBN 0-684-16381-0

This book published simultaneously in the
United States of America and Canada—
Copyright under the Berne Convention

All rights reserved. No part of this book
may be reproduced in any form without the
permission of Charles Scribner's Sons.

1 3 5 7 9 11 13 15 17 19 H/H 20 18 16 14 12 10 8 6 4 2

Printed in the United States of America

Thanks to...

When I was about halfway through this book, I started to think about the people to whom it should be dedicated: to my family and friends for all the right—but trite—reasons; to a high school teacher who taught me the meaning of education; to Oswald Cooper for designing the first typeface I was able to identify; or to the editor of a graphic design magazine who gave me support and advice when I needed it most.

When the book was completed, I realized the real thanks belongs to the people at Compugraphic Corporation. Not only did they set the type, prepare the illustrations, and produce the mechanicals, they also created an environment for my career growth in typography.

Thank you, Compugraphic.

A.H.

Contents

Introduction

The invention of movable type in 1450 ranks as one of the most important achievements in modern history. Movable type helped to bring humanity out of the Dark Ages and pave the way for advanced technology. With this development, centuries of knowledge and learning became available to anyone who could read. Educators, philosophers, scientists, and artists could now widely circulate their knowledge and learn from each other's experience.

Since 1450, type has changed and accelerated human development; however, until quite recently, the *technology* of movable type had changed very little. Over five centuries, refinements were made on the basic process: type became easier and less costly to produce, the image quality improved, ways were invented to make hand composition more efficient, and finally a means was devised to set metal type by machine. But the process itself didn't change until just after World War II. It was then that photography became a viable means of setting type, and a new revolution began.

Photography has made typography a convenient mass media. As a result of the photographic process, the cost of typography and typesetting equipment has dropped to a fraction of what it was a couple of decades ago. Consequently, typesetters are found in such diverse environments as small businesses, college campuses, churches, charitable organizations, postal services, insurance companies, research organizations, underground journals, hospitals, and television and radio stations.

As a result of more people becoming involved with typesetting, we are seeing more type. Those who predicted the electronic nonprint media would diminish the importance of print and the need for type were wrong. It has done exactly the opposite. There is currently a communications explosion, brought about by electronic technology and supported by phototypography. Type has become one of the most important and widespread communication media, and appears to be realizing more growth in its use within the last ten years than any of the other communications processes.

Most organizations involved with putting information on paper have a need for type, and it's now inexpensive enough to be easily cost justified as an in-house operation. In 1965 a linecaster matrix that yielded one metal typeface in one size cost approximately $1,000. Today, a piece of film, containing as many as four typestyles and producing a range of sizes from the small print on contracts to headlines an inch tall, can be purchased for approximately $200. Or to put it another way, if you were to purchase the same typographic capabilities from a metal linecaster from 1965 and a phototypesetter at current prices, the metal type would be 240 times more expensive!

Not only is type inexpensive, but it is designed to be an excellent communicator. Text type (main body type as opposed to headings) is created with *readability* and *legibility* as primary functions. Readability is measured by how easily and quickly copy can be read. Legibility refers to how easily one character can be distinguished from another; both are important factors in printed communication. The type designer not only creates beautifully rendered letters, but a system of communication in which each element is both distinctively different yet absolutely harmonious with all other parts—a system where aesthetic, optical, and mechanical factors are blended into a single unit. Type is one of those rare commodities where the total worth is more than the sum of its parts.

Type is also job oriented. There are typefaces created for every application. Faces are engineered for use at very small or very large sizes; there are condensed or narrow faces for parts lists and directories, and faces designed to attract attention, entice a reader into text copy, or create specific feelings and

SMALL

BOLD

Type for Every Need

Readability

Ease of Reading

Legibility

Character Recognition

BIG SALE
Important Bulletin
JULY PICNIC

Type to Call Attention

Newspaper Production

Social Stationery

MACHINE READABLE

Type for a Specific Purpose

THE NUMBER OF BOOKS dealing with lettering is fairly large, some going more or less into the history and develop ment of letterforms and others principally pre- sent models or facsimi-

Typewriter Type—10 Pitch

THE NUMBER OF BOOKS DEAL- ing with lettering is fairly large, some going more or less into the history and development of letterforms and others principally present models or facsimi- les of existing alphabets for suggestion or copying.

Typeset in English Times

More Copy with Typeset

moods. Typefaces have been designed specifically for newspaper production, for legal documents, social stationery, and business communication. There are even typefaces designed to be read by machines.

Because type is such an effective medium and typesetting machines are so proficient, it is predicted that typeset copy will someday replace typewritten copy in office environments. The total marriage of word processing and photo-typesetting may not happen as soon, or as easily, as many anticipate, but the two technologies are certainly going to be liv-ing together in the very near future. Not only is typeset copy between twenty to forty percent more readable and legible than typewritten copy, it saves space and is more likely to be read and remem-bered. As much as forty percent more copy can be set with phototypesetting equipment than with a typewriter. The cost saving becomes obvious: letters and documents that once took up one and one-half pages now fit nicely on a single sheet, postage costs drop, and filing space is substantially reduced.

With type, reports can be given the importance they deserve, and headlines can be added to vital communications to make them stand out in the pile of papers on a business desk. Technical in-formation is more accurate and under-standable with type.

Because of the current technological revolution in communications, we are literally entering a second Renaissance in type design and typography. It is a time of renewed excitement about type, and a time when new standards of excellence are being achieved.

The Basics

Parts of a character

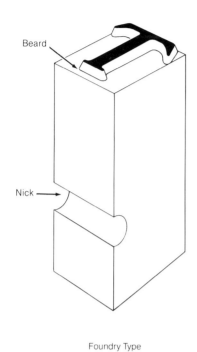

Foundry Type

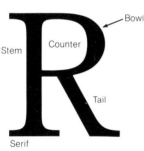

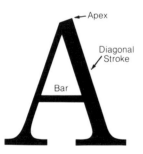

Reams of paper have been consumed describing and identifying the various parts of a letterform. As far back as the fifteenth century, writers were making up words to describe parts of letters to signmakers and calligraphers. Some of these early terms have survived until now, but most have not. The point is, in order to talk or write about type you have to have a language.

What follows is a condensed version of many previous lists of letterform nomenclature. Parts of a character not pertinent to current technology and usage have been omitted (a "beard" or "nick" was an important part of a foundry type character but have little relevance to phototype).

Arm
A horizontal stroke that is free on one or both ends.

Ascender
The part of the lowercase letters "b," "d," "f," "h," "k," "l," and "t" that extends above the x-height (the size of the lowercase x in any given typeface).

Bar
The horizontal stroke of the "e," "f," "t," "A," "H," and "T."

Bowl
A curved stroke that encloses a counter, except the lower portion of the lowercase "g."

Counter
Fully or partially enclosed space within a letter.

Descender
The part of the letters "g," "j," "p," "q," "y," "J," and "Q" that extends below the baseline.

Ear
The small stroke projecting from the right side of the upper bowl of the lowercase "g."

Hairline
The thin strokes in a serif type design.

Leg
The bottom diagonal on the uppercase and lowercase "k."

Link
A stroke connecting the upper bowl and lower loop of the lowercase "g."

Loop
The lower portion of the lowercase roman "g."

Serif
A line crossing the main strokes of a character. There are many varieties.

Shoulder
The curved stroke emitting from a stem.

Spine
Main curved stroke of the cap and lowercase "s."

Spur
A small projection from a stroke.

Stem
A vertical or diagonal stroke.

Stress
The direction of thickening in a curved stroke.

Stroke
A single straight or curved line.

Tail
A short diagonal stroke as in the uppercase "R," or parts below the baseline as in the lowercase "j" or "y."

Terminal
The end of a stroke not terminated with a serif.

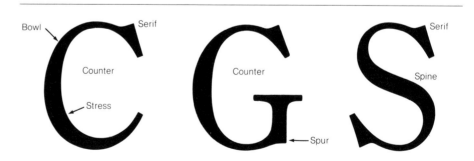

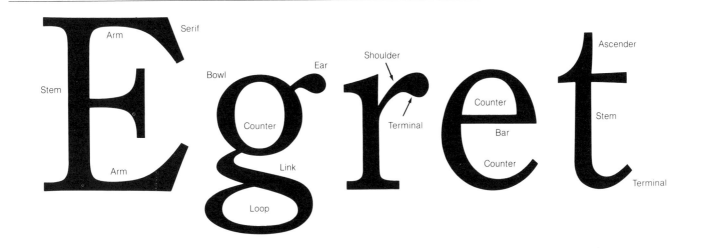

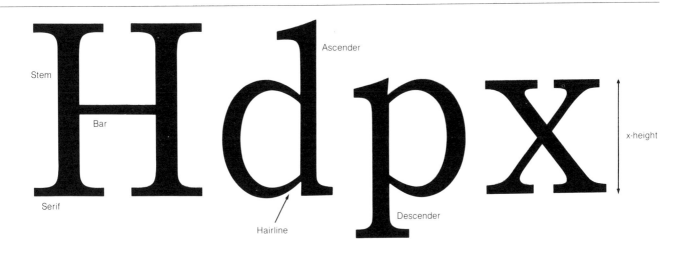

An alphabet is more than twenty-six letters

While a child may be taught there are twenty-six letters in the alphabet, the typesetter and typographer must be prepared to deal with many, many more. Within one typeface it is possible to have over 190 characters:

Capitals:

ABCDEFGHIJKLMNOPQRSTUVWXYZ&

Lowercase:

abcdefghijklmnopqrstuvwxyz

Small Caps:

ABCDEFGHIJKLMNOPQRSTUVWXYZ&

Ranging Figures:

1234567890

Oldstyle Figures:

1234567890

Superior (Superscript) and Inferior (Subscript) Figures:

1234567890 Figures 1234567890

Fractions:

$\frac{1}{3} \frac{1}{4} \frac{1}{2} \frac{2}{3} \frac{3}{4}$

Diphthongs:

ÆŒæœ

Ligatures:

ffl ffi ff fl fi

Math Signs:

$+ - \div \times = \% °$

Punctuation:

.·:,;!?·--""''"()[]/

Cap Accented Characters:

ÅÁÀÂÄÑÇ

Lowercase Accented and International Characters:

åáàâäñçøß«»¡¿

Reference Marks:

→ ᴿᴹ ᵀᴹ ℗ ® © □ ■ • * † ‡ §

Monetary Symbols:

$¢£

Typestyle classification

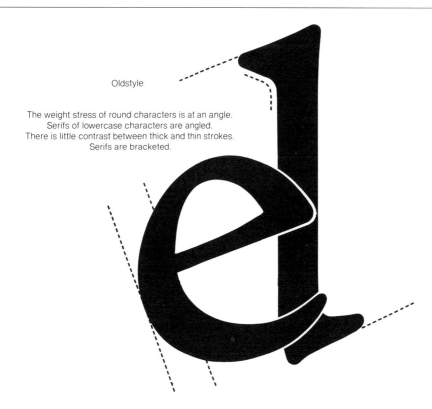

Oldstyle

The weight stress of round characters is at an angle.
Serifs of lowercase characters are angled.
There is little contrast between thick and thin strokes.
Serifs are bracketed.

Most of the typestyles designed can be divided into two classifications: those with serifs and those without serifs. Over the years, to further classify typeface design traits, several more definitive systems have been developed—some with over a hundred different categories.

A classification system can be helpful when trying to identify various typestyles, especially for the beginner. While two categories of type seem inadequate, hundreds become self-defeating. What is presented here are five main groups of typestyles; all other classification systems simply subdivide these. If you want a finer system, many are available to choose from; but this should be enough to get you started.

Oldstyle
Weight stress of round characters is at an angle.
Serifs of lowercase letter characters are angled.
Little contrast between thick and thin strokes.
Serifs are bracketed (connected to the stroke with a curve).

Modern
Weight stress of round characters is vertical.
Serifs of lowercase characters are horizontal.
Strong contrast between thick and thin strokes.
Serifs usually have little or no bracketing.

Slab Serif
Little or no weight stress.
Serifs are heavy and usually blunt.
Serifs are usually not bracketed.

Sans Serif
No serifs.
Strokes tend to be monotone in weight stress.
Characters tend to be geometric in design.

Script
Styled after handwriting.
Can have strong contrast in stroke weight, as if drawn with a quill pen, or very little, as if drawn with a brush.
Many letters are connected.

Modern

The weight stress of round characters is vertical.
Serifs of lowercase characters are horizontal.
There is strong contrast between thick and thin strokes.
Serifs usually have little or no bracketing.

Slab Serif

There is little or no weight stress.
Serifs are heavy and usually blunt;
they are usually not bracketed.

Sans Serif

There are no serifs.
Strokes tend to be monotone in weight stress.
Characters tend to be geometric in design.

Script

Script is styled after handwriting.
It can have strong contrast in stroke weight, as
if drawn with a quill pen, or very little, as if drawn with a brush.
Connecting letters appear frequently.

What is x-height?

x-Height

One of the first things I wanted to learn in my high school algebra class was: "What does "x" equal?" I quickly learned that "x" can equal anything. The same thing happened with typography. One of my initial questions was "How much is an x-height?" Same answer: anything. The x-height refers to the size of the lowercase "x" in any given type-face at any given point size. It is actually a proportional description of a typeface.

Typefaces are generally size classified by point size (which is basically a mea-sure of the tallest part of the alphabet above the baseline to the lowest part below). However, since over ninety-five percent of all letters read are lowercase characters, and the proportion of the characters will vary from typeface to typeface, the x-height is an important factor. It refers to the size of the vast majority of typographic characters read.

Seemingly similar typefaces may have very different x-height proportions. Futura's lowercase characters are quite small when compared to those of Helvet-ica, and Antique Olive's x-height is larger than either Futura's or Helvetica's. In serif designs, Times Roman is con-sidered to have a large x-height while Bembo's x-height is usually referred to as small.

In new display type designs the current trend is toward a very large x-height. For example, the lowercase in Americana is over eighty percent of the capital (cap height), while the average for text faces is between fifty percent and sixty-five percent.

Large x-heights generally make a typeface more visible at any given point size. Thus, display faces with excep-tionally large lowercase characters may communicate their message with clarity and emphasis. The text typefaces that incorporate large x-heights do so in an attempt to increase legibility and readability.

Times Roman, created specifically for the London *Times* newspaper, has a large x-height to aid in reading. It was designed with a larger x-height than previous book faces (which were at one time used in newspapers) since newspapers are generally held at a greater distance from the eye than books. Bembo, on the other hand, was designed for text setting in books and therefore does not require the large lowercase size.

Although in some situations a large let-ter size may be preferred, "The Bigger the Better" is not always appropriate typographic philosophy. There is a price to pay for all this visibility and readabil-ity—as the x-height increases, the number of characters that can be set in any given space decreases. For example, in any given measure ten percent more copy can be set in Futura Medium than in ITC Avant Garde Gothic Medium. When you consider a ten percent longer book or a ten percent increase in adver-tising space, the cost of visibility and readability becomes very apparent. Faces with a small x-height can, in some in-stances, be more readable than those with a large lowercase. *Note:* If you are setting many lines of text copy with no additional line space, the proportionally longer descenders and ascenders of a typeface with a short x-height will create the illusion of more white space between lines of type.

What does all this mean to you? Simply that you should be aware of the demands and requirements of the job to be type-set, and try to use the typeface of correct proportions.

As with most things in typography, there are no pat answers or absolute rules governing the choice of typeface with various x-heights. By being atten-tive to the kinds of jobs you are doing and aware of the type library available to you, you're taking the first steps toward proper typeface usage.

FuturaxxHelveticaxxAntique Olive

x-Height Comparisons of Sans Serif Typefaces

Times RomanxxBembo

x-Height Comparisons of Two Serif
Typestyles

Americana Hx

x-Height over 80%
of the Capital Height

Plantin Hx

Average x-Height for
a Text Typeface

The number of books dealing with lettering is now fairly large, some going more or less deeply into the history and development of letterforms while others principally present models or facsimiles of existing alphabets for suggestion or copying.

10-Point Antique Olive
Set Solid

The number of books dealing with lettering is now fairly extensive, some going more or less deeply into the history and development of letterforms while others will principally present models or facsimiles of existing alphabets for suggesting or copying.

10-Point Futura Medium
Set Solid

Bembo
Garamond
Caledonia
Electra

Book Typestyles: Generally
Smaller x-Heights

The number of books dealing with lettering is now fairly extensive, some going more or less deeply into the history and development of letterforms while others will principally present models or facsimiles of existing alphabets for suggesting or copying.

12-Point Futura Medium

The number of books dealing with lettering is now fairly large, some going more or less into the history and development of letterforms while others principally present models or facsimiles of existing alphabets for suggestion or copying.

12-Point ITC Avant
Garde Gothic Medium

21

Type families

Mountain

Old Style Antique

Homes

Catalogue Antique

Forest

Bookman

Three Names of One Typestyle

Cheltenham Oldstyle

Cheltenham Wide

Cheltenham Medium

Cheltenham Bold

Cheltenham Bold Condensed

Cheltenham Bold Extra Condensed

Cheltenham Bold Outline

Cheltenham Oldstyle Condensed

Cheltenham Italic

Cheltenham Medium Italic

Cheltenham Bold Italic

Cheltenham Bold Condensed Italic

CHELTENHAM BOLD EXTRA CONDENSED TITLE

Cheltenham Bold Extended

Cheltenham Extrabold

Cheltenham Inline

Cheltenham Inline
Extended

Cheltenham Inline
Extra Condensed

Cheltenham Family

Although the idea of a type family has been around for over one hundred years, it took Morris Fuller Benton of American Type Founders Company to popularize the concept. In the late 1800s, the American Type Founders Company was formed through a merger of over twenty independent type founders. Each company had a type library of hundreds of typestyles, many of which duplicated styles in other companies. The task of standardizing this massive typographic resource became the responsibility of Morris Benton. In an attempt to organize the typestyles, he grouped all the designs with similar traits under a generic name. Thus, Old Style Antique and Catalogue Antique, two faces of the same design from two separate manufacturers, both became Bookman, and Thorne Fat Face eventually became Ultra Bodoni because of its many similarities with the Bodoni typestyles.

In addition, American Type Founders began to release new typestyles within family groupings. While some families were complete at the time of release, other typeface families continued to grow as a response to customer demand. The Cheltenham family is a good example of the latter. It grew from the two faces of the original release in 1904, to a family of twenty faces eight years later.

Since the advent of phototype technology, complete type families can now be planned and designed before any faces are actually produced.

A type family consists of a number of typefaces which show a marked resemblance, but have individual design variances, such as weight, proportion, angle, and surface texture.

Weight

The most common and obvious variation within a type family is weight. Typestyles can range from very light to extremely heavy stroke widths and still maintain family design traits. There is a British standard that classifies stroke weight changes in eight gradations: *extra light, light, semilight, medium* (usually the parent weight of the family), *semibold, bold, extra bold,* and *ultrabold.* Two other common weights not covered under the British standard are book, a midpoint between light and medium, and black, which is usually considered bolder than ultrabold. There are also many other names, such as fat, slim, hairline, elephant, and massive, to describe type family weight changes. There are even some families (Univers was one of the first) that use a numerical code to distinguish typeface weights.

Proportion

Character proportion is another variation on a family theme. By various stages, typestyles can be condensed or proportionally expanded from the parent design. Standard proportional increments are known as *ultra condensed, extra condensed, condensed, normal, expanded, extra expanded,*

Futura Light

Futura Book

Futura Medium

Futura Demibold

Futura Bold

Futura Extrabold

Family Weights

and *ultra expanded.* Other terms are also common, especially with display typestyles. Condensed proportions are sometimes referred to as *compressed, elongated,* or *narrow,* while expanded designs in some type families are classified as *wide, extended,* or *stretched.*

Angle

The design that results from changing the angle of a typestyle is called *italic.* This variation includes both simple oblique letters and a true cursive design. Originally, italic letters were not part of a type family. They were created as an independent design, based on formalized handwriting, to save space in the sixteenth-century version of our paperback books. Many years passed before the italic typeface was included as part of the type family, and many more before it was actually designed as a complement to the roman face.

Italics based on classic handwriting are generally called *cursives,* and have an almost script quality to them. Cursive designs are almost exclusively confined to serif typestyles. Obliques appear to be just slanted letters and are usually the italic designs of sans serif typefaces.

Surface Texture

Surface texture is another variant within a type family. There are outline designs, typestyles that have the appearance of three dimensionality, incised, stenciled, textured, and comstocked typefaces. There are even reverse typefaces designed as a time-saver for production artwork.

The point to remember about the members of a typeface family is that although they may be varied and diverse, they all maintain the basic characteristics of the parent design—in much the same way that a single piece of music can have several arrangements.

Latin Bold Condensed

Latin Bold

Latin Wide

Family Proportions

Obliqued

Slanted Roman Design

Cursive

Based on Classic Handwriting

OUTLINE

THREE DIMENSIONAL

Incised

STENCIL

TEXTURE

Comstock

Reverse

Family Textures

univers 45
univers 55
univers 65
univers 75

Weights Indicated by Numbers

Points and picas

dg

72 Points
25.3 mm

The technology of typesetting has been around for about five hundred years, and yet it has only been within the last century that printers and typographers have had a standard measuring system. Prior to standardization, there were as many systems to measure type as there were type founders. Mixing types from several founders often proved to be a difficult, if not impossible, task.

At first, type sizes were given names rather than a logical numerical coding system. One of those names, agate, is still used in the newspaper industry; it refers to the 5½-point type used for setting classified ads. Other names such as *brilliant, diamond, nonpareil, minon, bourgeois,* and *long primer* sound romantic and quaint, but were troublesome to use and to interrelate.

The first logical, uniform measuring system for type was developed by the French in the eighteenth century. It is called the didot system after the foundry which helped establish it, and is still used in Europe. The American system for type measurement was established over a hundred years after the French and is based on a somewhat smaller measurement than the didot.

In the American system, which is also used in England and Australia, the smallest unit of measure is called a *point*. A point equals .0138 inch or approximately one-seventy-secondth of an inch. Purists will argue that there are not exactly 72 points to an inch, and they are correct, but this relationship is close enough for most measurements. Points are generally used to determine small vertical measurements such as the size of type or the amount of white space between lines. The next larger measuring unit is called a *pica* and is equal to 12 points.

1 American point   = .0138 inch
1 American point   = .351 mm
12 American points = 1 American pica

Picas are used to measure larger, usually horizontal dimensions such as line lengths. The term pica is taken from the old-fashioned name for type that size.

In the didot system the smallest unit is also called a point. It is, however, slightly larger than an American point.

1 didot point = .0148 inch
1 didot point = .375 mm
1 didot point = 1.07 American points

The next larger unit is again comprised of 12 points. Twelve didot points are called *cicero* in Germany, Austria, and Switzerland, *douze* in France, *riga typographia* in Italy, and *augustijn* in Holland. Fifteen ciceros equal approximately sixteen picas.

We are now experiencing the introduction and development of yet another type measuring system: metric. With photographic and computer technology, the choice of measuring standards can be somewhat arbitrary. But, because the metric system is fast becoming universal, it is only natural that it be incorporated into typography, and a plan to do so has been in effect since 1964. Although American acceptance is still a few years off, some manufacturers of phototypesetting equipment are already including a metric counting system as part of their machine hardware.

Ems, Ens and Thins

Other units of measurement are called *ems, ens* and *thins*. These units were originally pieces of type, shorter than the printing surface, used to add space between printed elements. An em was equal to the square of the point size. Thus a 12-point em was 12 points high by 12 points wide, an 8-point em was 8 points high by 8 points wide, and so on. An en space was one-half the width of an em, and a thin space was usually considered to be one-fifth as wide as an em. With phototype these sizes have changed slightly—for the better. Ems, ens, and thins are now generally typeface sensitive. This means that the em space in a condensed typeface, such as Univers Light Condensed, will take up less space than an em in an expanded typestyle. This enables spacing to be proportional to the design of the typeface. The result is better typography. En spaces and thin spaces are, of course, still proportional to the em space of the particular typestyle. An en remains one-half the width of the em space. However, to facilitate the setting of tabular matter, the thin space has been changed, in many cases, from one-fifth of the em to one-half of the en or one-quarter of the em.

In metal type, thins, ens, ems, and longer spaces called quotations, were used for almost all spacing, from paragraph indentations and interword spacing to line justification and centering. With phototype, these are now simple machine functions.

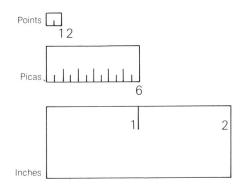

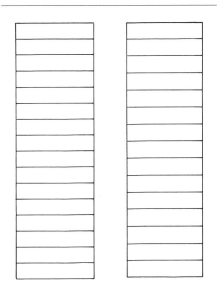

16 Picas   15 Ciceros

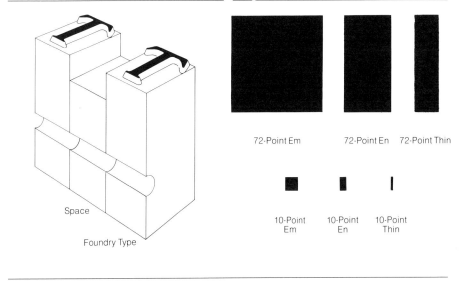

Space

Foundry Type

72-Point Em   72-Point En   72-Point Thin

10-Point Em   10-Point En   10-Point Thin

Univers 47

Univers 47 Em

Univers 53

Univers 53 Em

What is a unit?

Balmy

26 Units 17 Units 8 Units 27 Units 18 Units

Avant Garde

18-Unit System

Avant Garde

54-Unit System

A unit in phototypesetting is the basic interface between the design of the letterform and the mechanics of the phototypesetter. Unit systems are based on the em which is the square of the point size. When creating typefaces for phototypesetting, the type designer must render an aesthetically pleasing character that is also contained within a number of the units in the em. When type is set, the phototypesetter exposes the character, then moves the number of units (width assignment) of the character before exposing the next character.

While many manufacturers of phototypesetting equipment work within an 18- or 36-unit-to-the-em system, a 54-unit system is the most flexible. The greater number of units gives the type designer more latitude in character-width assignment.

The finer grid system does not necessarily aid in converting the standard "bread and butter" text typefaces from metal to photographic typesetting; most of these were originally cast in metal to a 9- or 18-unit system.

However, the more flexible system does allow new typefaces, which may not have been designed within unit system confines (faces such as ITC Avant Garde Gothic), to be added to phototype libraries with little or no character reproportioning. More important, it allows the phototypesetter to utilize, on a single image carrier, typefaces of varying proportions or designs (from super condensed to extra expanded), thus providing more typographic flexibility than ever before possible.

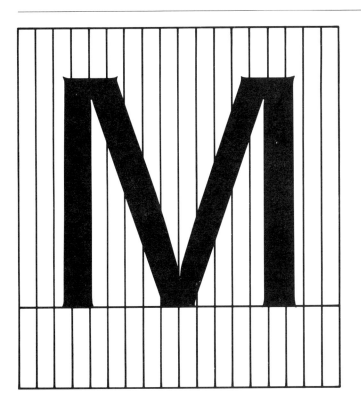

18-Unit

54-Unit

Unitizing Grids

Text and display—what is the difference?

The number of books dealing with lettering is fairly large, some going more or less into the history and formation of letterforms, while some present models or facsimiles of existing alphabets for suggesting or copying.

Example of Dazzling

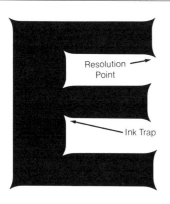

Resolution Point

Ink Trap

Text

Display

Most manufacturers of phototypesetting equipment offer both text and display character designs. Text type, drawn from 6 to 12 point, is used primarily for setting body type (type used for reading matter). Display characters range from 14 to 72 point and are generally used for advertisements, title pages, and part and chapter headings.

Having both kinds of type will give you maximum flexibility in meeting specific typesetting requirements. As to when to use which kind of type, the following description of actual design differences will help you make these decisions.

Character Proportions

Type and typography are visual media. Characters are proportioned to make the machine output appear optically the same at various point sizes. In serif typefaces, for example, the thin parts of a character are designed proportionally heavier for text designs than for display. If they were left the same weight as the display design, the contrast between thick and thin would be too great, causing an effect called "dazzling," which makes the copy difficult to read.

The interior spaces of characters are more open in text designs to allow the eye to easily distinguish character differences. In text designs, the lowercase characters are generally taller in relation to the cap height than their display counterpart (again to aid the eye in reading). Thus, display designs usually will have proportionally larger descenders than text.

In sans serif designs, *resolution points* are added to the corners of characters; in areas where two strokes meet, some weight is taken out. This is to keep the letters crisp and sharp through the photo reproduction processes necessary in off-set printing. In text faces these points and lightened areas are more pronounced.

Character Spacing

Text designs generally have more inter-character spacing than display. A properly spaced line of display type at 60 point would look much too tight and difficult to read if reduced to 10 point.

Tabulation

The points, numbers, and various signs of text designs are *tabular*, that is, they share common width values. This enables you to easily set tables and columns of numeric characters for annual reports, time tables, or catalogue listings. Display typefaces are not necessarily tabular and can be difficult to use in columnar work.

The degree to which display and text designs are dissimilar varies from type family to type family. Only you can determine if the degree of difference will have an effect on your work.

Why, Then, Are Some Typefaces Recommended for Both Text and Display?

A combined text and display design usually occurs when the typeface is monotone in nature and does not require the alteration of thicks and thins for contrast. This is not true of all monotone designs, as original type foundries still prefer to tighten letterspacing and add weight when converting display to text sizes.

In many typefaces, however, the conversion was taken into account in the initial phases of design, and compromises were made so spacing would not be too loose in display or too tight in text.

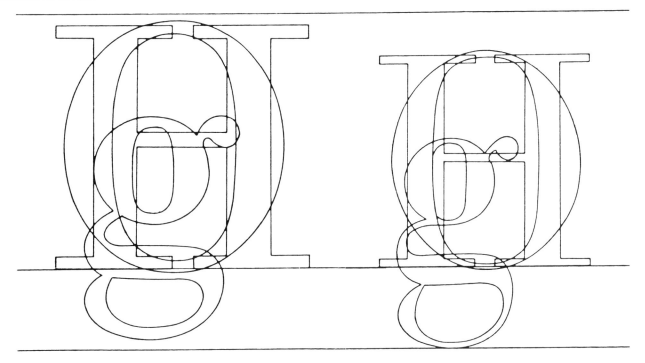

Text

Display

champion

Text

champion

Display

Spacing Differences Between
Text and Display Designs

21320048
38009990
12000886
11151231
34557279

Text

ITC Benguiat Book

24 Point

ITC Benguiat Book

10 Point

Text and Display Design

21320048
38009990
12000886
11151231
34557279

Display

Copyfitting and Copy Preparation

Copyfitting: making type fit the space

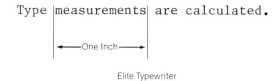

Elite Typewriter

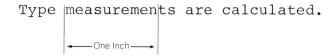

Pica Typewriter

Copyfitting is the process of establishing how much space typewritten copy will occupy when converted to typeset copy. Copyfitting is absolutely essential when working with type, since it makes no sense to set copy in a particular typeface and size if you aren't certain it will fit into the intended space. Because there are so many mathematical calculations involved in computing character-per-pica information, copyfitting often is a confusing process.

Copyfitting involves three basic measurements: *inches, picas,* and *points.*

The inch is a unit of measurement that is a part of our day-to-day lives. We measure in inches everything from a piece of paper to the scale of a road map.

Determining the number of characters in a typewritten manuscript (the first step in copyfitting) is not unlike determining the number of miles represented on a map. To find out how many characters a manuscript contains, you must first determine the scale or the number of characters per inch.

Each character in a typewritten line occupies the same amount of space. For example, the small ''i,'' the capital ''T,'' punctuation, and spaces between words are all the same width. The difference is in the size of the characters typewriters generate. Fortunately, most typewriter characters fall into the two size groups of *pica* and *elite.* Of the two, the pica typewriter has the larger character, allowing ten characters to an inch; the smaller character on the elite typewriter measures twelve characters per inch.

Type measurements are calculated in smaller units called points and picas.

The smaller unit is the point. A point is equal to one-seventy-secondth of an inch, that is, there are seventy-two points to one inch. The larger unit is the pica. There are six picas to an inch, or 12 points to one pica.

The area the type will occupy is measured in picas and points. Although pica values will eventually be converted to points during copyfitting procedures, it is easier to record the width and depth of an area in this larger unit of measurement.

Character-Counting Text Material

Text copyfitting begins with a typewritten manuscript. You must determine how many characters are in the copy before it can be converted to typeset composition. This procedure is called *character counting*. Because it would take an endless amount of time to count each character in a large manuscript, a simple method, based on characters per inch, is used to arrive at a character count.

You may not always know which typewriter was used to prepare the manuscript: a pica typewriter generating ten characters per inch or an elite typewriter producing twelve characters per inch. This can be determined by counting the number of characters, spaces, and/or punctuation that occupies one inch. Because interword spaces and punctuation appear in the final typeset copy, it is important to include them in the character count.

After establishing the number of characters per inch, draw a vertical line along the right margin of the manuscript at the width of an average line. Measure the line to the nearest inch and multiply this figure by the number of characters per inch. Add any remaining characters to the total. For example, a line typed on a pica typewriter measuring five inches will contain fifty characters. If one additional character remained in the line, the total number of characters would be fifty-one. A line typed on an elite typewriter and measuring five inches will yield sixty characters. If one character remained in the line, the total number of characters would be sixty-one.

The average line is used as a basis to count the number of characters of an entire page or manuscript. When dealing with a lengthy manuscript, check all pages for deletions or additions and make sure different typewriters were not used since these factors will affect the count.

Count the number of lines on the page. Multiply this number by the number of characters in the average line to derive an approximate count. If a more accurate accounting is important, add all the characters that extend beyond the vertical line, and subtract any characters that fall short of it.

If you do not want to count every page of a lengthy manuscript, you can do a character count of what you would consider an average page and multiply this number by the total number of pages. Again, this will only be an approximate count. Do not let the large numbers scare you. After a while, you will be accustomed to thinking in terms of hundreds of thousands of characters (especially in book design).

```
Copyfitting is the process of establishing how much
space typewritten copy will occupy when converted
to typeset copy. Copyfitting is absolutely essential
when working with type since it makes no sense to
set copy in a particular typeface and size if you are
not certain it will fit into the intended space. There
is something about copyfitting that scares and con-
fuses people, probably because there are so many mathe-
matical calculations and research involving character
per pica information. To simplify this research, a
chart for each machine group is given in this bulletin
listing the character per pica information. Each
chart contains the required typographic data for all
Compugraphic typefaces in both text and display designs.
```

Average Line:
51 Characters

$$
\begin{array}{r}
51 \\
\times\,14 \\
\hline
714
\end{array}
\begin{array}{l}
\text{characters per line (average)} \\
\text{lines contained in manuscript} \\
\text{average number of characters in manuscript}
\end{array}
$$

COPY SPECIFICATIONS
Type Style: Helvetica
Point Size: 10 point
Line Measure: 22 picas

DATA COLLECTED
Characters Per Pica: 2.4
Character Count: 714 characters

$$\begin{array}{r} 22 \\ \times\,2.4 \\ \hline \mathbf{52.8\ or\ 53} \end{array}$$

22 pica measure
× 2.4 characters per pica
52.8 or 53 typeset characters per line

Characters Per Pica

You will also need to know the characters-per-pica information for the particular typeface and point size in which the copy or manuscript is to be set. As the name implies, characters-per-pica values refer to the average number of characters that will fit into the length of a pica.

Most manufacturers of phototypesetting equipment publish characters-per-pica values for the faces in their type library. *Note*: Do not use the characters-per-pica values published by one manufacturer to calculate the typefaces of another. Just as type designs vary slightly from manufacturer to manufacturer, so do characters-per-pica values.

If published charts are not available, a close approximation can be obtained by measuring the length of the lowercase alphabet (from a to z) in points, and using the following formula:

$$\frac{\mathbf{342}}{\text{lowercase alphabet (in points)}} = \text{characters per pica}$$

Converting Typewriter Copy to Type

The appearance of the final typeset composition should be considered before copyfitting procedures are continued. You should know the style of type, the size, and the line length to be used. This information is often specified in advance, making your job an easy one. However, in some cases, such as in ad composition, type must be restricted to a given area. You must then select a size and style that enables the copy to fit into the area indicated in the design layout. Several stages of "trial and error" may be required before the right style and size are chosen.

To find the total number of lines the manuscript will occupy in a given type style and size, multiply the characters-per-pica figure by the selected line length to determine how many characters will fit into one typeset line. When necessary, round off any decimal remainder to the next highest value. Divide the total number of manuscript characters by the number of characters per line. Your answer is the number of typeset lines contained in

13 typeset lines
—————————————————
53 | 714 character count in manuscript

the manuscript. Because it is an estimate, you may find a slight difference between the actual typeset copy and your calculations. This is normal and to be expected.

The above calculations are based on the assumption that the type was set *justified* (lines aligning both left and right). If type is to be set *ragged* (lines aligning on one side only), you estimate the number of characters per line by using the length of an average line. For example, if you specify that the longest line is to be twenty picas and the shortest is to be sixteen picas, then the average line will be eighteen picas.

Line Space Calculations

The depth per page that typeset lines occupy can be determined by multiplying the number of lines by the point size. Since this total depth, specified in points,

```
  13   typeset lines
× 10   point type
─────
 130   points = depth of type
```

is cumbersome, it should be converted to picas, just as inches are converted to feet for clarity. This is accomplished by dividing the total number of points by twelve.

10 picas and **10** points
—————————————————
12 | 130 points depth of type

After determining the depth of type, it is often necessary to space out the lines to fill a given area. Because space between lines, known as line space or leading, is measured from the baseline of one line of type to the baseline of the line that follows, the last line requires no line space and only the point size is considered in this calculation. Therefore, to define the

amount of line space required, subtract the point size from the total depth of the specified areas. Because this takes into

```
  14   picas, depth of copy
× 12   points per pica
─────
 168   points total depth
```

account the height occupied by the point size of the last line, divide this figure by one less than the number of lines calculated. This number is the required line space value.

13 points of line space
—————————————————
12 | 158

What if your type doesn't fit into the specified area?

The number of books dealing with lettering is now fairly large, some going more or less deeply into the history and development of letterforms while others principally present models or facsimiles of existing alphabets for suggestion or copying.

Basic Paragraph 10 Point 11 Point Linespace

The number of books dealing with lettering is now fairly large, some going more or less deeply into the history and development of letterforms while others principally present models or facsimiles of existing alphabets for suggestion or copying.

10 Point 10 Point Linespace

The number of books dealing with lettering is now fairly large, some going more or less deeply into the history and development of letterforms while others principally present models or facsimiles of existing alphabets for suggestion or copying.

9 Point 11 Point Linespace

The number of books dealing with lettering is now fairly large, some going more or less deeply into the history and development of letterforms while others principally present models or facsimiles of existing alphabets for suggestion or copying.

Typeface with Fewer Characters Per Pica

The number of books dealing with lettering is now fairly large, some going more or less deeply into the history and development of letterforms while others principally present models or facsimiles of existing alphabets for suggestion or copying.

Line Measure Increased by 6 Points

After doing all these calculations, you may find that your type doesn't fit into the allotted area: you may have too much type or not enough. In either case, you have several options.

The most obvious solution is to reduce or increase the point size, allowing the line measure and line space to remain the same. Fortunately, this does not require re-copyfitting the entire job since type is sized proportionally through the photo-typesetter's lens systems. For example, if the point size were reduced from 10 to 9 point, the job would occupy ten percent less space or be ninety percent of its original depth. The line space may also be altered to gain additional space when necessary. If the original job specified 10-point type with 11 points of line space, the length of the finished piece could be altered by reducing line space, or the same point size/line space ratio could be maintained by setting 9-point type with 10 points of line space.

If the point size cannot be changed, it is often necessary to select a different style of type. If a style containing fewer characters per pica is selected, the copy will occupy more space than the originally specified face.

In some instances, the design layout may permit you to increase or decrease the line measure. As few as 6 points will make a difference in the amount of vertical space the type will occupy.

Line space calculations for mixed point sizes

Unlike the uniform leading or line spacing found in text composition, line space values must be varied when point sizes are mixed from one line to another. For example, additional line space is required between a headline and the text that follows to allow for the descenders of the larger point size. A guideline for determining the correct line space value is based on adding one-third of the larger point size (the space occupied by the descenders plus white space) and two-thirds of the smaller point size (the space occupied from the baseline of type to the top of the highest ascender). These two values added together represent the minimum amount of line space between two different sizes of type.

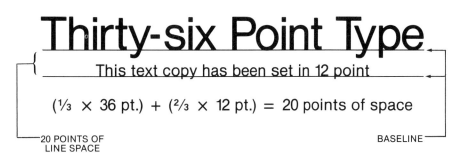

$$(⅓ × 36 pt.) + (⅔ × 12 pt.) = 20 \text{ points of space}$$

20 POINTS OF LINE SPACE

BASELINE

Copy mark-up

9/10 Century Old Style

14 picas

☐Once you · have determined the typestyle, point size, line spacing, line length, and other typographic spec-ifications, the next step is to mark these typesetting instructions on the manu-script. This process is called <u>copy mark-up</u>.
☐The appropriate information should be written with a ball-point pen, colored pencil, or felt-tip marker to separate it clearly from the copy to be typeset. Instruction should be ligible, precise, and allow no chance for misinterpre-tation.

Once you have determined the type-style, point size, line spacing, line length, and other typographic specifications, the next step is to mark these typesetting instructions on the manuscript. This process is called *copy mark-up*.

The appropriate information should be written with a ballpoint pen, colored pen-cil, or felt-tip marker to separate it clearly from the copy to be typeset. Instructions should be legible, precise, and allow no chance for misinterpretation.

Use of accepted proofreaders' marks and an accompanying rough layout will ensure that the finished piece will match your intended design.

Note: The number of handwritten cor-rections in a manuscript is directly pro-portional to the increased chance for typesetter error. Also, most typesetting houses charge extra for working with "dirty" copy.

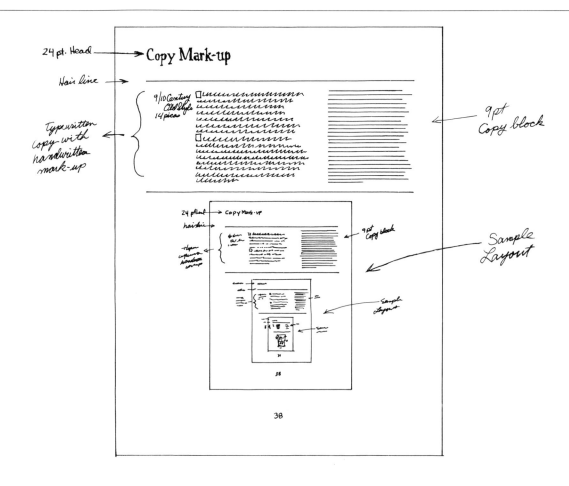

24 pt. Head

Hair line

Typewritten copy with handwritten mark-up

9 pt Copy block

Sample Layout

Proofreaders' marks

Proofreaders' marks are the symbols used to indicate changes, additions, and deletions to typeset copy.

Some of the marks are done directly on the typeset copy, others in the galley or page proof margin. In the margin a slash mark (/) follows the suggested change or addition or deletion; when several changes are made in the same line, it is especially important to separate them by slash marks.

Symbol	Meaning
# ⓧ#	Insert space.
⁀	Close up or tighten space, or bring together.
/	Separate these words or materials or sentences.
1/M	Insert or set as em dash.
1/N	Insert or set as en dash.
=	Insert or set as hyphen.
(and)	Enclose in parentheses.
[and]	Enclose in brackets.
eq#	Equalize spacing.
ℊ	Delete copy.
∧	Insert copy at desired place in text.
◯	Change or question copy circled.
◯ Rom	Set copy in roman typestyle.
___	Change underlined characters to italic typestyle.
═	Set copy in small capitals.
≡	Set copy in capital letters.
/ or lc	Make characters marked lowercase.
∿ or bf	Set copy in boldface type.
lf	Set copy in lightface type.
‖	Align copy vertically.
═	Align copy horizontally.
[ ]	Move copy horizontally.
⊓ ⊔	Move copy vertically.
(SP)	Spell out.
∿	Transpose words or letters.
¶	Begin new paragraph.
No ¶ or ⊃	No paragraph; copy should run continuously.
∨"	Insert quotation marks.
∨'	Insert single quotation marks or apostrophe.
∨*	Insert asterisk.
∨†	Insert dagger.
∨3	Insert indicated superior character.
∧3	Insert indicated inferior character.
⊙	Insert period.
∧,	Insert comma.
(:)	Insert colon.
∧;	Insert semicolon.
∧?	Insert question mark.
∧!	Insert exclamation point.
stet	Let it stand; disregard all marks.
□ or [1]	Indent one em space.
□□ or [2]	Indent two em spaces.
□□□ or [3]	Indent three em spaces.

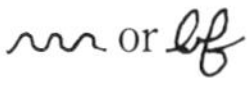

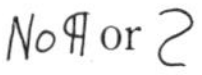

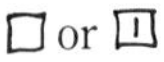

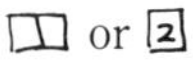

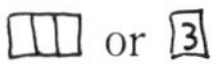

Getting Started

Building a type library

Times Roman
Times Roman Italic
Times Roman Bold
Times Roman Bold Italic

Needed from Times Roman Family

There are three times when you need to be concerned with acquiring new fonts: (1) When you purchase your initial piece of typesetting equipment; (2) When you want to increase your business; (3) When you want to keep from losing business.

Selecting Initial Fonts

Purchasing your first typesetter will carry with it the responsibility to select fonts. To choose among the staggering array of typefaces can be difficult, especially since your knowledge of type may not be as sophisticated as it will soon become.

It is best to start out "small" with your initial type purchase—just buy the minimum number of fonts you will need in order to get by. You can always order more later. The possible penalty you pay for not ordering everything on the "quantity discount plan" that most manufacturers offer will be offset by the assurance that you won't be stuck with a font, or fonts, you don't need.

Order by family. Unless you have a specific purpose to do otherwise, purchase typefaces in a family grouping. Ordering your type in this way will allow you to make systematic and logical additions to your library at a later date. If you have a hodgepodge of typestyles, it is difficult to use them as an effective foundation for a larger library.

If you own a typesetter that utilizes filmstrips or disks containing more than one typeface, there are other important reasons to order by family. First it makes ordering easier. Manufacturers of these style image carriers have the members of a family already made up in logical combinations. By ordering families, you can take advantage of quantity discount plans.

Image carriers made up of type family variants are easier to use than those with scattered typeface combinations. For example, you might want to set a job with text copy in Univers Light and Univers Light Italic, with running heads in ITC Korinna Bold and a title headline in ITC Korinna Heavy. If the Univers variants are on one image carrier, but, for one reason or another, the two Korinna weights are on two separate image carriers, you've committed yourself to setting part of the job, changing the machine dress, setting the remainder of the job, and finally an unnecessary paste-up process. All this is time consuming and costly.

Grouping of family variants on a single image carrier, rather than three or four faces from different families, will also help you refrain from using awkward typeface combinations within a single job just because they are there. All the members of a type family are of compatible design, so you can mix them at will with little fear of poor typographic combinations.

Anytime you order type, but especially on your first order, do your homework! Know the exact faces you want and why. Avoid letting a machine sales representative work out your entire order for you.

The bare minimum for your first type order should be twelve typefaces.

Four faces from the Times Roman family:

Times Roman
Times Roman Italic
Times Roman Bold
Times Roman Bold Italic

This family is the most used and the most popular typestyle in existence today. It is suitable for almost any composition; to attempt to list Times Roman applications would only serve to put limits on a type family that seems to have none. It is a "must" for every typesetter's library.

And eight faces from the Helvetica family in the basic weights of:

Roman
Italic
Bold
Bold Italic

Plus:

Light
Light Italic
Condensed
Bold Condensed

Helvetica (or whatever the particular manufacturer calls it) is the most popular sans serif style in use today. With these weights you can set almost any basic text matter, create running heads, advertising copy, parts lists, directories, etc.

Roman
Italic
Bold
Bold Italic
Light
Light Italic
Condensed
Bold Condensed

Needed from Helvetica Family

ITC Souvenir
Palatino
Optima
Stymie
Script

Important Typestyles

Baskerville
Caledonia
Century
Garamond
Goudy Old Style
Univers

Publishing Typestyles

Other faces that would be applicable to general typesetting, and could be included in your first order, would be:

ITC Souvenir
Palatino
Optima
Stymie
one script

With these, and the Times and Helvetica families, you'll have: the most used serif typestyle; a large, usable sans serif family; the most popular ITC design; the "pretty" Palatino; Optima—a transition between serif and sans serif; a square serif; and a script.

Adding to Your Library

The time to buy type again is when you have a better idea of where you are going with your enterprise, when you feel more confident about your type needs, when you want to increase business by expanding the resource for the service you provide, or when you believe you are losing business you want to a nearby competitor with a larger type library.

On succeeding type orders, fill out the existing families you have, especially the ones you are using the most. Building a type library is like purchasing a good set of tools (the tools of your trade). To have a full complement of a particular tool makes normal jobs easier and difficult jobs manageable.

The first step should be to round out the Helvetica family. Add extrabold weights and extended designs. Helvetica is a good, strong backbone on which to base the remainder of your library.

The next faces to add should be popular or alternate designs for the kind of service you provide. If your business is primarily text composition for publishing or related fields, concentrate on adding more classic book faces:

Baskerville
Caledonia
Century (either textbook or expanded
   —although Old Style is a good
   alternative)
Garamond
Goudy Old Style
Univers (an alternative to Helvetica)

If your work is more advertising oriented add the versatile ad faces:

ITC Avant Garde Gothic
ITC Korinna
ITC Kabel
ITC Serif Gothic
ITC Tiffany
Antique Olive
Gill Sans
Goudy Old Style
Futura

Versatile advertising typefaces have a distinctive design that separates them from other typestyles, and yet are conservative enough to use in a variety of applications. A study of popular consumer magazines will tell you which typefaces are most popular. Don't order a new typestyle if you've only seen it used once or twice.

A minimum-sized type library will contain twelve faces from the Times Roman and Helvetica families. A large commercial library that could handle most jobs will contain about one hundred faces from approximately twenty-four typeface families. If you plan to become a trade typographer you can expect to have at least two hundred to two hundred and fifty typefaces in your library.

A type library is an investment in the future of your business; treat it with the same respect and care you would any investment. Add to the resource only when the business climate warrants it, and don't hesitate to ask for counseling.

ITC Avant Garde Gothic
ITC Kabel
ITC Korinna
ITC Serif Gothic
ITC Tiffany
Antique Olive
Futura
Gill Sans
Goudy Old Style

Advertising Typestyles

The right type for the right job

Helvetica Condensed
Univers Medium Condensed

Good Space Savers

Helvetica Condensed is one of the many typefaces available for your use. Careful attention to its design characteristics in relation to other faces will help you to choose the right face for any job.

Helvetica Condensed Used in Copy

SANS NO.1 is one of the many faces that is avail able for your use. Caref ul attention to the design characteristics in relati onship to other faces wi ll help you to select the right typeface for any job.

DIRECTORY GOTHIC is one of many typefaces available for use. Careful attention to its des ign characteristics in comparis on to other faces will enable you to choose the right face for any job.

For Small Sizes Only

If you are working professionally with type, either by setting it or specifying it, you are practicing the art of typography —the art of arranging words and images for the communication of ideas through the medium of printing. The key word is "communication." If you work with typography, you are also a communicator. The better you prepare your message, the more likely it will be read, understood, and remembered. This brings the "art" of typography down to a very practical level: the effectiveness of your printed pieces directly relates to you and your company's success as communicators.

One of the easiest, and most obvious, ways to create good typography—effective communication—is to use the correct typeface for each job. This is a simple task if you are aware of the application of the job and the type library available. You must make logical choices, taking these two aspects into account. Basically, the task is not a difficult one. The following guidelines will help you make these choices.

If Space Is at a Premium (In Catalogues, Parts Lists, Etc.)

Not only is the wise use of space stressed in this kind of work, clarity is also vitally important. You want to get as much information as possible in a given space, and it must be highly readable. The logical choice is one of the condensed sans serif typefaces; News Gothic Condensed, Univers Medium Condensed, or Helvetica Condensed are all good selections. Although News Gothic Condensed has the shortest lowercase alphabet length of the three families, enabling more copy to fit in any given space, it also has a smaller x-height that can inhibit readability. On the other hand, Helvetica Condensed has the longest lowercase alphabet length, but it is the easiest to read. The lowercase alphabet length of Univers 57 falls in the middle.

The best all-around choice is Helvetica Condensed. It is the most legible condensed design of the three families, and even though it has slightly fewer characters per pica than Univers Medium or News Gothic, the loss of copy space is negligible.

If space is at an absolute premium, there are several families, such as Directory Gothic or Sans No. 1, which are designed to be used in very small point sizes and still remain highly readable. It should be noted, however, that these two families are generally unsuitable for use above 7 or 8 point.

The Copperplate family is another possibility, although its design (two sizes of capital letters in the same size of type) can limit its application.

Advertising Pieces
(From Shoes to Sailboats)

You have two important goals in advertising typography: to catch the viewer's attention, and once you've got it, provide easy-to-read information.

Bold, extrabold, and black are good weights to use for headlines to catch the viewer's attention. Variations such as condensed sans serif faces, which allow you to pack more words into a given space, can be used effectively, too. Faces with a drop shadow, such as Uncle Sam Open or Pioneer, are also good choices since the illusion of dimensionality attracts notice.

The use of highly decorative or unusual typeface designs should be avoided. While they may catch the reader's eye, they are usually low on the readability scale. If the reader can't get past the headline, the text of the ad certainly will not be read.

The informative part of the advertisement—the part you want the viewer to read and remember—should be set in a conservative text design. A serif typeface usually works best if the headline has been set in sans serif. While Times Roman is often the best choice, two good alternatives are Goudy Old Style and ITC Korinna Regular. Both are currently very popular typefaces and their distinctive designs enhance many kinds of advertising.

COPPERPLATE LIGHT IS ONE OF MANY FACES AVAILABLE FOR YOUR USE. CAREFUL ATTENTION TO ITS DESIGN CHARACTERISTICS IN RELATION TO OTHER FACES WILL ENABLE YOU TO SELECT THE RIGHT TYPEFACE FOR ANY JOB.

Copperplate Used in Copy

UNCLE SAM

OPEN

PIONEER

Attention Getters

ITC KORINNA is one of the many typefaces available for your use. Careful attention to its design characteristics in relation to other typefaces will enable you to decide on the correct typeface for any job.

GOUDY OLD STYLE is one of the many typefaces available for your use. Careful attention to its design charact eristics in relation to other faces will enable you to choose the correct typeface for any job.

Popular Advertising Text
Typefaces

MIQUE
THUNDERBIRD EXTRA CONDENSED
NEW BOSTONIAN

"The Good Old Days"

Palatino
Palatino Italic
Americana
Americana Italic
Trump Mediaeval
Trump Mediaeval Italic

Classic Beauty

Quill
Uncial
LIBRA
Cartier

Calligraphic Feel

If you choose a sans serif typeface for the text, it should be a conservative design, such as the medium weights of Helvetica and Univers. However, to give an advertisement a little distinction, consider ITC Avant Garde Gothic.

Mood Pieces
(Menus, Invitations, Programs, Etc.)

In designing mood pieces, you are trying to evoke empathy in the reader. For example, not only do you want to advertise a circus, you also want to give the reader a feeling for the fun and spirit associated with it.

It is in this kind of work that a library of decorative typefaces is an asset. With the following styles at your disposal, you'll be prepared for ninety percent of the mood pieces you may be asked to do:

Faces that conjure up the feeling of the old West, or "the good old days," faces implying "classic beauty."

Faces that achieve a calligraphic effect.

For certain moods, there is Old English, but be careful—this face is used far too much! Cloister Black, a more distinctive design, is a good alternative.

Period faces like LSC Manhattan can say "1920s" while Computer tends to evoke a futuristic feeling.

Lengthy Text Settings (Books, Magazine Articles, Etc.)

The decision process is somewhat more difficult in selecting text type. The face must be very effective at conveying information. It must be readable and should not interfere with the process of giving information. In short, the reader should be able to see through the type as though it were invisible.

Inevitably, when discussing the selection of typefaces for lengthy text material, the argument is raised as to which is the better choice of typestyles, serif or sans serif. Contrary to traditional opinion, sans serif type can work equally as well as the serifed typeface designs. The argument used by traditionalists is that sans serif type in text material is not as readable as the serifed faces. The fact is, when shorter line lengths are used, sans serif typefaces are read just as easily as serifed typefaces.

The two sans serif "workhorses" are Univers and Helvetica; they are both excellent choices for sans serif text settings.

Although Helvetica has a slightly larger x-height than Univers, as well as a longer lowercase alphabet length, text copy set in Univers can be less tiring on the eyes since it has a thick and thin quality to the letters as opposed to the more even strokes of Helvetica. For this reason, Univers could be the better choice for lengthy text settings.

Other sans serif faces suitable for text matter are ITC Avant Garde Gothic, Futura, and News Gothic; however, few of these measure up to the design quality and readability of Univers and Helvetica.

Whether sans serif will eventually replace serif typefaces is debatable. Serif faces have been around for a long time and continue to serve their purpose—to aid the reading of medium to long lines. And there are more serif typefaces from which to choose.

The more modern serif typeface designs work very well for lengthy text work. For the most part, they have a larger x-height and are compatible with offset printing. Goudy Old Style is a very good choice for many kinds of work since it is very legible and has its own unique qualities.

ITC Souvenir, especially the light, is also a good typeface.

The Times Roman and Century Schoolbook families are the most popular serifed typefaces. You can't go wrong using them.

One last thing should be mentioned: there are no absolutes in typography. These guidelines are basic aids to help you determine the right typeface for a particular job; they should not be considered hard and fast rules. Awareness of the vast type resources available and choosing with care will make your selection as valid as anyone else's. The most important points to consider are the purpose of the final printed piece and the use of contemporary typography as an art to achieve effective graphic communication.

Old English Cloister Black

- Period Faces

Manhattan COMPUTER

Mood Faces

Univers is one of the numerous ty pefaces available for use. Careful attention to its design characterist ics in relationship to other styles will enable you to choose the right typeface for any job.

Helvetica is one of many typefac es available. Careful attention to its design characteristics in rela tion to other faces will enable you to choose the right typefac es for any job.

Sans Serif Workhorses

GOUDY OLD STYLE is one of the many typefaces available for your use. Careful attention to its design charact eristics in relation to other faces will enable you to choose the correct type-face for any job.

Modern Serif Typeface

CENTURY SCHOOLBOOK is one typeface of many available for your use. Careful attention to its design characteristics in relati on to other faces will enable you to choose the right typeface for any job.

TIMES ROMAN is one typeface of many available for your use. Caref ul attention to its design characterist ics in relation to other faces will ena ble you to choose the right typeface for any job.

Serif Workhorses

ITC SOUVENIR LIGHT is one of the many typefaces available for your use. Careful attention to its design ch aracteristics in relation to other typefa ces will enable you to decide on the correct face for any job.

A Good Text Typeface

Good Text Typography

Proper line length, line spacing, and interword spacing

Serif Typestyle

9–10 Words per Line

Sans Serif Typestyle

7–9 Words per Line

The number of books dealing with lettering is now fairly extensive, some going more or less deeply into the history and development of letterforms while others will principally present models or facsimiles of alphabets for suggesting or copying.

Poor Line Breaks

The selection of the typeface and point size are important typographic decisions that affect the utility and/or mood of a printed piece. Typographic quality, however, is achieved by proper usage of line length, line spacing, and interword spacing.

In order to use these typographic elements correctly, you must consider many factors. Perhaps the most important factor is the application, which usually determines the selection of a typestyle and point size. Different kinds of typesetting require different typographic specifications. For example, booklets or newsletters can have longer lines than photo captions or advertisements because they are read at arm's length and, usually, more thoroughly. However, if the reader is meant to capture the message quickly or read the message from a distance, a shorter measure is strongly recommended. The fewer pauses the eye is forced to make, the faster a line can be read. In short lines, the selection of words and how they break at the end of a line are important factors, since each pause required by the eye should make sense to the reader.

To determine the remaining typesetting specifications, it is important to analyze the design characteristics of the selected typeface:

- Is the typeface serif or sans serif?
- Does it have a large or small x-height?
- Do the letterforms have strong thick and thin contrasts or are the letters designed with uniform strokes?

By answering these questions, you will be able to establish the correct relationship of the selected typeface to line length, line spacing, and interword spacing.

Line Length

A correct line length is one that:

- Complements the typeface and point size used.
- Supports the intended application of the piece.

Contrary to what many think, the eye does not read individual words, one at a time, but scans the line pausing momentarily to record groups of three or four words. The easier it is for the eye to do this, the more effective communication becomes. Too long a line length tends to tire the eye and interferes with referencing the beginning of the line that follows. On the other hand, lines that are too short can be difficult to read since sentence structure is often broken.

If the typeface you're using is a serif design, a line containing an average of nine or ten words is generally considered the proper line length. Since serifs serve to aid the eye's horizontal movement across the page, sans serif faces generally require a slightly shorter line length for maximum readability. A line containing approximately seven to nine words is considered to be the proper length for most sans serif designs. Problems that can develop from setting too long a line in a sans serif typeface can be seen in the following example:

The number of books dealing with lettering is fairly large, some going more or less deeply into the history and development of letterforms while others principally present models or facsimiles of alphabets for suggestion or copying.

Line Too Long for Sans Serif Style

Resetting the same block in a serif typestyle using the same point size makes the paragraph below easier to read.

The number of books dealing with lettering is now fairly large, some going more or less deeply into the history and development of letterforms while others present models or facsimiles of alphabets for suggestion or copying.

Reading Made Easier Set in
Serif Typestyle

Typefaces with larger lowercase x-heights, like ITC Souvenir and Times Roman, permit longer line lengths than smaller x-heights found in Bembo or

Futura. Because over ninety-five percent of the characters read are in lowercase, the larger the proportion of the lowercase letter to the cap height and point size, the more legible they become. In short, the easier they are to read.

The length of the text block is also an important factor to consider. For example, the small x-height of Bembo is much more readable in extended text settings than Antique Olive, which has a very large x-height. If possible, look at a specimen of a typeface before using it in any application. This will help you determine if it will accomplish your intended purpose.

Faces with a strong thick and thin contrast, such as Bodoni or ITC Tiffany, require shorter line lengths; they can be difficult to read in extended settings, creating a "picket fence" appearance that tires the eye.

Line Spacing

The amount of space inserted between lines of type directly affects the legibility of the printed piece. Proper line spacing creates a thin horizontal strip of white between lines of type that serves as a guideline for the eye. When there is too much white space between lines, reading becomes slower, legibility is inhibited, and the job becomes longer, costing more to produce.

A general rule for achieving proper line spacing is that it should be approximately twenty percent of the point size in use. For example, the proper line spacing for 10-point type would be two extra points (i.e., 12 points of line space). This is, however, just a rule-of-thumb. There may be many times when you will not want to, or be able to, maintain a strict twenty percent line space. Line space values fluctuate depending on application and typeface. Remember that you want to avoid both a lengthy job and doubling (the tendency to read the same line twice).

The current trend in typesetting seems to be toward adding only 1 point of line space regardless of the application or typestyle used. This can cause serious problems especially if you are working with an excessively long line (fourteen words or more).

Compare the two examples of 8-point type. Each copy block contains lines of

The number of books dealing with lettering is now fairly large, some going more or less deeply into the history and development of letterforms while others principally present models or facsimiles of existing alphabets for suggestion or copying.

The number of books dealing with lettering is now fairly large, some going more or less deeply into the history and development of letterforms while others principally present models or facsimiles of existing alphabets for suggestion or copying.

More Line Space for Heavy
Typefaces

The number of books dealing with lettering is now fairly large, some going more or less deeply into the history and development of letterforms while others principally present models or facsimiles of alphabets for suggestion or copying.

Word Space Larger Than Line Space

ULTRA-THIN BLACK LEADS—
0.5mm (0.20") thick.

Medium—	U6-603-14-6	
Medium Hard—	U6-603-16-6	
Tube of 18 leads.		75¢

THIN BLACK LEADS—
(.036") thick.

Soft—	U6-603-23-6	
Medium—	U6-603-24-6	
Medium Hard—	U6-603-26-6	
Tubes of 24 leads.		40¢

THIN COLORED LEADS—0.9mm
(.036") thick.

Red—	U6-600-24-6	
Green—	U6-600-22-6	
Blue—	U6-600-21-6	
Yellow—	U6-600-26	
Tube of 12 leads.		40¢

No Extra Line Space Needed

The number of books dealing with lettering is now fairly large, some going more or less deeply into the history and development of letterforms while others principally present models or facsimiles of existing alphabets for suggestion or copying.

The number of books dealing with lettering is now fairly large, some going more or less deeply into the history and development of letterforms while others principally present models or facsimiles of existing alphabets for suggestion or copying.

A short x-height makes Bembo (top)
appear to have more line space.

The number of books dealing with lettering is now fairly large, some going more or less deeply into the history and development of letterforms while others principally present models or facsimiles of existing alphabets for suggestion or copying.

The number of books dealing with lettering is now fairly large, some going more or less deeply into the history and development of letterforms while others principally present models or facsimiles of existing alphabets for suggestion or copying.

Heavier typefaces may need more line space.

The number of books dealing with lettering is now fairly extensive, some going more or less deeply into the history and the development of letterforms while others will principally present models or facsimiles of alphabets for suggestion or copying.

The number of books dealing with lettering is now fairly extensive, some going more or less deeply into the history and the development of letterforms while others will principally present models or facsimiles of alphabets for suggestion or copying.

Light typefaces can be set solid.

Idealiwordispaceiisiaboutitheiwidthiofitheiletter i.

Ideal word space is about the width of the letter i.

Ideal word space is about the width
of letter "i" and its surrounding white space.

approximately fourteen words. The first block has only 1 point of line space and is far more difficult to read than the second block, which has 2 points of line space.

Although the general rule for correct line spacing is to use a value that is twenty percent of the point size, less line spacing may be advisable in the following situations:

- When lines contain eight words or less.
- When setting reference material, parts lists, directories, and catalogues, space is at a premium.
- When the typeface has a small x-height.
- When light weights of a typeface are being used.

Greater line spacing values may be advisable in the following situations:

- When lines contain fourteen words or more.
- When the typeface has a large x-height.
- When the visual texture or color of the page becomes darker through the use of heavier weights of a typeface.

Typeface design plays an important part in selecting the correct line spacing. Since short x-heights create an appearance of more white space between lines, faces such as Bembo or Gill Sans can require less line space than the larger x-heights found in Times Roman or Helvetica.

As the visual texture, or color, created by type becomes darker, reading becomes more difficult. The readability of heavier faces such as Antique Olive or ITC Korinna is enhanced by using more space between lines to lighten the color of the page. On the other hand, light faces such as Baskerville or Univers 45 require less space between lines.

Some blocks can be set *solid*, which means that the line spacing value is equal to the point size. Care should be taken, however, that the space between words does not appear larger than the space between lines, as illustrated in the exemplary copy block.

Although solid set composition is usually not recommended for most text applications, it can be very beneficial for materials that are not read continuously. Reference works, directories, parts lists, and catalogues, where space is usually at a premium, are all applications that could require no additional line spacing. With the aid of bold headlines, the reader can easily seek information on a line-for-line basis without interrupting the communication process.

Word Spacing

Word spacing is probably the single most important factor contributing to good typography and effective communication, yet its true importance is seldom acknowledged. Although most phototypesetters have a minimum and maximum word spacing adjustment, simply programming these values is not enough.

When too much space appears between words, the line breaks into separate elements, inhibiting reading. A quick check to determine if the typeset composition contains too much word space is to turn it upside down. If you can easily distinguish one word from another, the word spacing is too wide.

A good rule to follow: the ideal space between words should equal the width of the letter "i" of the typeface and point size being used. The maximum should not exceed the width of an en space. Incorrect use of word spacing becomes especially apparent in text composition where the space between words is greater than the space between lines. The shorter the measure, especially in justified copy, the more difficult it is to control word spacing.

Word spacing should be proportional to the point size and typeface being used. For example, most sans serif designs will require tighter word spacing than a serif typeface since they lack the benefit of serifs to aid the eye's horizontal movement across the page. Most condensed faces need tighter word spacing to produce the even color (or texture) created by the type. Faces with a smaller lowercase x-height may also require tighter word spacing.

Wider word spacing may be advisable when using an expanded design or a typeface that has a larger lowercase x-height. Also, certain techniques, such as reverse type, require wider word spacing for legibility.

The amount of word spacing may be affected by:

- The difference between serif and sans serif design.
- The difference between condensed and expanded typefaces.
- Line spacing.
- Line measure.
- Justified or unjustified typesetting.

Although many guidelines can be stated regarding the proper use of line length, line spacing, and interword spacing, there are exceptions to most rules. Careful consideration of these elements combined with a little common sense will make the finished piece inviting to the eye and easy to read.

The number of books dealing with lettering is now fairly extensive, some going more or less deeply into the history and development of letterforms while others will principally present models or facsimiles of existing alphabets for suggestion or copying.

Poor Word Space

The number of books dealing with lettering is now fairly large, some going more or less deeply into the history and development of letterforms while others principally present models or facsimiles of alphabets for suggestion or copying.

Good Word Space

The number of books dealing with lettering is fairly large, some going more or less deeply into the history and the development of letterforms while others principally present models or facsimiles of existing alphabets for suggestion or copying.

The number of books dealing with lettering is fairly large, some going more or less deeply into the history and the development of letterforms while others principally present models or facsimiles of existing alphabets for suggestion or copying.

Too tight word spacing in reversed copy makes reading difficult.

To justify or not to justify

UIT a pueɹo diuae Viɹginis cultoɹ eximius, cui ſtatas quotidie pɹeces ſolitus eɹat peɹſolueɹe. Verum quia inſtabilis et nutabunda eſt puerilis pietas, coepit et in eo larioribus velis pia haec conſuetudo nauigare. Pedetentim igitur ſolitas orationes atque ſuffɹagia, primo ad unum diem, dehinc ad duos aut tɹes, demum ad qua-

One of the most fiercely argued questions in typography is whether justified composition is better than unjustified. Justified composition is text copy that has been set with the lines of type flush, or aligned on the left and right margins, while unjustified copy has flush left margins with an uneven or nonaligning right margin. One faction of typophiles will tell you that justified composition aids readability, is more pleasing to the eye, and generally is better typography. Another faction will tell you that unjustified is better—for the same reasons! The truth is: neither one is inherently better typography.

Justified and unjustified composition are both equally readable, and can be good (or poor) typography depending on how they are handled. An interesting note is that readers are almost never aware as to whether they are reading justified or unjustified copy.

Why the controversy? Because both can cause typographic problems if handled poorly, and many experts choose to believe the problems are intrinsic to the typesetting style. If you are aware of the possible problems and avoid them, you can set beautiful and effective typography justified or unjustified.

Justified Typography

If you prefer justified typography you have tradition on your side. Gutenberg's Bible (the first use of movable type) was set with all lines flush left and right. The even blocks of type give a neat, orderly appearance to the page, which is preferred by many people. In addition to being traditional, justified composition can be easier to produce. With the typesetter in a justified mode, an operator does not have to make line-ending decisions. The machine's logic determines where to stop the line and automatically adjusts the interword and/or inter-character spaces to equal the predetermined measure.

One major problem with setting justified copy is running the risk of creating excessive interword spacing. Many times the typesetter is presented with remaining space on the line, but not enough to set the next word or a hyphenation of it. Therefore, the word ends up on the next line causing the previous line to be spaced out with additional interword spacing. The result can be too much word spacing. Justified, short line measures are especially difficult to set. A look at most newspaper columns will show you excessive word space and "rivers" of white running through the copy.

The longer the line measure the less this problem occurs. Books and magazines that are set justified have tighter word spacing since they generally use wider columns of type. If you are setting justified composition within a narrow column, often word spacing problems can be corrected by increasing or decreasing the line measure slightly.

Unjustified Typography

The biggest advantage of unjustified typesetting is the ability to control word spacing. You can have tight, even word spacing in any length line, and, as mentioned earlier, good word spacing is probably the single most important factor in high-quality, effective typography.

Another advantage is that making corrections often is easier. Ragged right lines allow the possibility of adding or subtracting a few characters or even a word without seriously affecting the typographic quality. This is not possible with justified typesetting.

The disadvantage of unjustified typesetting is that it can be difficult to produce and still remain high-quality typography. Very long lines followed by very short ones can cause awkward shapes that are not inviting to the eye. Ideally, unjustified composition should appear to be optically justified. This means that the operator must make all the end-of-line decisions and spacing adjustments. Therefore, the typographic quality will be only as good as the machine operator.

Paragraphing can also cause problems. If the copy being typeset has a number of short blocks containing paragraph indents, the finished piece can look as though it was set ragged left and right.

Which is more desirable? Only you can answer this depending on your personal preference and the particular job application. Either will reward you with high-quality, effective typography. Be wary of excessive word spacing when setting justified and very uneven line lengths when setting unjustified.

The number of books dealing with lettering is now fairly extensive, some going more or less deeply into the history and development of letterforms while others will principally present models or facsimiles of existing alphabets for suggestion or copying.

Justified

The number of books dealing with lettering is now fairly extensive, some going more or less deeply into the history and development of letterforms while others will principally present models or facsimiles of existing alphabets for suggestion or copying.

Unjustified

Columbus, OH—Training, motivating management and personnel currently are the greatest obstacles to using electronic mail systems, according to researchers.

In a recent study on future uses for electronic mail systems directly—without going through secretaries—is expected to be a major barrier to their proper use. Electronic mail includes the generation, transmission, storage, disposition, and display of business correspondence and documentation by electronic means.

Rivers

Kerning

To

Spacing Defined by Units

To

Not Kerned

To

Kerned

Kerning is the selective reduction of white space between two letters. Type is designed so that each character has optimum spacing relationships with every other character. To accomplish this each character is designed within a specific space. In metal and wood type this space is defined by the edges of the block on which the character sits. In phototype the space is determined by the establishment of a unit, or width, value.

Kerning characters in handset type was a difficult and time-consuming process. It involved either cutting off a small amount of the metal on the type to be kerned (which ruined the type for regular composition), or using specially designed alternate characters that fit snugly and actually overlapped the surrounding type.

In phototypography the process of character kerning is much easier and is also done in one of two ways. With the more difficult of the two (which really isn't difficult), the keyboard operator must be aware of which letter combinations need to be kerned. When one of these combinations is encountered, the operator simply removes a little white space through a keystroke. The other method requires no action on the part of the operator. Several phototypesetting systems offer, as an option, preprogrammed kerning capabilities. The operator just types the copy, and the phototypesetter knows which characters are to be kerned and how much. This process is also typeface sensitive in that the kerned characters and amount of white space removed are adjusted from typeface to typeface.

Is kerning necessary to good typography? Probably not. It does create an even color, or texture, in text composition, and, in some cases, it increases legibility. Kerning in text sizes is a nice touch: it looks attractive, and says something about the care with which the typography was assembled. However, as type sizes become larger, kerning becomes more necessary to produce even letterspacing, and to improve readability and legibility.

What follows is a table of common kerning pairs: letter combinations that under normal typesetting conditions can produce uneven or awkward spacing.

While the basic procedures of typography remain the same for all type sizes, and the basic design characteristics of a typestyle do not change drastically as its size increases, display type is a slightly different typographic commodity than text type. As type sizes increase, the elements of good typography shift slightly to more emphasis on individual letterforms and their relation to surrounding positive and negative space, rather than the texture created by groups of letters.

What follows is background information and some basic guidelines for handling display type.

AC AL AN AO AT AV AW AY

Av Aw ac af ao at au av

aw ax ay

CA CO CT CY Co Ce

DY du

ew ex ey

FA FG FO F, F. Fa Fe Fo Fu

GY

KE KO ke ko ku

LA LI LL LO LS LT LV LW LY

Ma mu

NT nu

OA OT OV OW OY

PA PE PO PR P, P. Pa Pe Po Pr

Qu

RA RO RV RY ra rc re ro

SA ST SY sys st

TA TC TE TO TS TW TY T, T.

Ta Te To Tr Tu Tw Ty

VA VO VY V, V. Va Ve Vo

WA WO WV WY W, W. Wa We

Wh Wi Wo Wr wa we w, w.

YA YO YS Y, Y. Ya Ye Yo

ya ye yo ys y, y.

ZA

Kerning Pairs

Never mix, never worry: which typestyles can be mixed and which cannot

Goudy
Old Style
ITC Tiffany

Avoid mixing typestyles with
pronounced curves or large serifs.

Eurostile
Extended

**Bodoni
Condensed**

Contrasting shapes are seldom good mixers.

Helvetica

Univers

Two sans serifs seldom mix well.

The axiom about being careful with the combination of various alcoholic concoctions holds true with typography. Mixing the wrong typographic ingredients can also result in dire consequences. Several typeface combinations can produce inharmonious designs. If two or more typestyles are used for a particular job, they should be of complementary designs whenever possible.

Typography should have cohesiveness and utility. These qualities will make your work more attractive to look at, generally easier to read, and certainly better communication.

- Typestyles with pronounced curves, exaggerated serifs, or other outstanding characteristics (like Goudy Old Style or ITC Tiffany) should not be mixed indiscriminately.
- Typefaces with extremely contrasting shapes, such as Eurostile Extended or Bodoni Condensed, are seldom good combinations.
- Mixing two sans serif designs is generally not a good idea; especially if they have similar design traits like Helvetica and Univers.

The following matrix provides general guidelines for typestyle mixing. Display typestyle choices are listed across the top, and text choices are down the side. To determine typestyle compatibility, cross-reference from horizontal to vertical. The number in the box that intersects two typestyles will indicate the degree of compatibility. The numeral one indicates complete typestyle compatibility (mix at will). Combinations intersecting with a numeral two should be handled with caution. Typestyles that intersect at a numeral three should be avoided.

1 OK
2 Be Careful
3 Avoid Like Plague

	Text
	Alternate Gothic
	Americana
	Antique Olive
	Avant Garde Gothic
	Baskerville
	Bauhaus
	Bembo
	Benguiat
	Bodoni
	Bookman
	Caledonia
	Caslon
	Century Expanded
	Century Old Style
	Century Schoolbook
	Cheltenham
	Cooper
	Eurostile
	Franklin
	Friz Quadrata
	Futura
	Garamond
	Gill
	Goudy Old Style
	Helvetica
	Kabel
	Kennerley
	Korinna
	Melior
	News Gothic
	Optima
	Palatino
	Quorum
	Romana
	Scripts
	Serif Gothic
	Souvenir
	Souvenir Gothic
	Stymie
	Tiffany
	Times Roman
	Trump Mediaeval
	Univers
	Weiss
	Windsor
	Zapf Book

Display	Alternate Gothic	Americana	Antique Olive	Avant Garde Gothic	Baskerville	Bauhaus	Bembo	Benguiat	Bodoni	Bookman	Caledonia	Caslon	Century Expanded	Century Old Style	Century Schoolbook	Cheltenham	Cooper	Eurostile	Franklin	Friz Quadrata	Futura	Garamond	Gill	Goudy Old Style	Helvetica	Kabel	Kennerley	Korinna	Melior	News Gothic	Optima	Palatino	Quorum	Romana	Scripts	Serif Gothic	Souvenir	Souvenir Gothic	Stymie	Tiffany	Times Roman	Trump Mediaeval	Univers	Weiss	Windsor	Zapf Book
	1	1	3	3	1	3	1	1	1	1	1	1	1	1	1	1	2	3	2	1	1	2	2	1	2	2	1	1	3	2	1	2	1	2	2	1	2	1	1	1	1	1	3	1	1	1
	1	1	1	1	1	1	1	2	2	2	2	2	2	1	2	2	3	1	2	1	1	2	1	1	1	1	1	2	2	2	1	2	1	3	2	1	2	1	2	3	1	1	1	2	2	2
	3	1	1	3	1	3	1	1	1	1	1	1	1	1	1	1	3	3	2	1	2	1	3	3	1	1	1	3	2	1	2	1	3	1	1	2	1	1	1	1	1	3	1	1	1	1
	3	1	3	1	1	3	1	1	1	1	1	1	1	1	1	1	3	3	1	3	1	2	1	2	1	2	2	1	2	1	1	1	1	1	3	1	1	1	1	1	1	3	1	1	1	1
	1	3	2	2	1	2	2	3	1	3	3	3	3	3	3	2	2	2	1	3	1	2	1	1	2	3	3	1	1	3	1	2	1	1	2	1	3	3	3	2	1	3	3	2
	3	1	3	3	1	1	1	1	1	1	1	1	1	1	1	1	2	3	2	1	2	1	2	1	2	2	1	1	1	2	2	1	2	2	1	1	1	1	1	1	1	2	1	1	1	1
	2	3	2	2	3	3	1	3	3	3	3	3	3	3	3	3	2	2	2	3	1	2	1	1	2	3	3	1	2	3	1	3	3	3	2	1	3	3	3	2	1	3	3	2
	3	2	1	1	1	1	1	1	2	2	2	2	1	2	2	1	1	1	1	1	2	1	1	1	2	2	1	1	1	3	1	1	1	1	2	2	2	2
	2	3	1	2	2	2	3	3	1	2	3	3	3	3	3	3	2	2	2	1	2	1	2	1	1	2	2	1	2	2	1	2	1	2	2	2	2	1	3	3	3	2	1	2	3	3
	1	2	1	1	1	1	1	2	1	1	1	2	2	2	2	2	1	1	1	1	3	1	1	1	2	2	1	1	2	1	2	2	1	2	1	2	2	1	1	2	2	2
	2	3	1	1	2	2	2	3	3	3	1	3	3	3	3	3	2	2	2	2	3	2	2	1	3	3	3	2	1	3	2	3	1	2	2	2	3	3	3	3	1	3	3	3
	2	3	1	1	2	2	2	3	3	3	3	1	3	3	3	3	2	2	2	2	3	2	3	1	1	3	3	3	2	1	3	2	3	1	2	2	2	3	3	3	3	1	3	3	3
	1	3	1	1	2	2	3	3	3	3	3	3	1	3	3	3	2	2	2	2	3	2	3	1	1	3	3	3	2	1	3	2	3	1	2	2	2	3	3	3	3	1	3	3	3
	1	2	1	1	1	1	2	2	2	3	2	2	2	1	1	2	3	1	1	1	2	1	2	1	1	2	2	1	1	2	1	1	1	2	1	2	3	2	3	1	2	2
	1	2	1	1	2	2	2	2	2	3	2	2	2	2	3	3	3	2	2	2	1	3	1	2	1	1	2	2	3	1	2	1	2	2	2	2	1	2	3	2	3	1	2	2
	1	2	1	1	1	1	2	2	2	2	1	2	1	1	1	1	2	1	1	1	1	2	1	1	1	1	3	2	1	1	2	1	2	2	1	1	3	2	1	2	1	2	2
	1	1	1	1	1	1	1	1	1	1	1	1	1	1	1	1	1	1	1	1	1	1	1	1	2	2	1	1	2	1	2	1	2	2	1	3	1	2	2	1	1	1	2	2	2
	2	1	3	3	1	3	1	1	1	1	1	1	1	1	1	1	3	1	3	1	2	1	3	3	1	1	1	3	3	1	2	1	2	2	1	2	1	1	1	1	1	3	1	1	1
	3	1	3	3	1	3	1	1	1	1	1	1	1	1	1	1	3	1	3	1	3	1	3	3	1	1	1	3	3	1	2	1	2	1	1	2	1	1	1	1	1	3	1	1	1
	2	2	2	2	1	2	1	1	1	1	1	1	1	1	1	2	1	2	1	1	1	1	1	1	2	2	1	2	1	2	1	3	1	1	1	1	1	1	1	1
	3	1	3	3	1	3	1	1	1	1	1	1	1	1	1	1	3	2	1	1	3	1	3	2	1	1	1	3	3	1	2	1	2	1	1	2	1	1	1	1	3	1	1	1
	2	2	1	1	2	1	3	2	3	3	3	1	2	3	2	3	2	2	2	1	1	1	2	1	2	2	1	1	2	1	2	2	2	2	1	2	3	2	2	1	3	2	2
	3	2	3	3	1	3	1	1	1	1	1	1	1	1	3	3	1	1	1	3	3	1	1	1	3	3	1	2	1	2	1	2	1	1	1	1	1	1	1	3	1	1	1
	2	3	1	1	3	3	3	3	3	1	3	3	3	3	2	2	1	2	2	3	2	3	2	1	3	2	3	1	2	3	2	2	3	2	3	2	2	3	3
	3	1	3	3	1	3	1	1	1	1	1	1	3	1	1	1	1	1	1	1	3	2	1	2	1	2	1	1	2	1	1	1	3	1	1	1
	3	1	3	2	1	3	1	1	1	1	1	1	1	1	1	3	1	3	1	3	1	3	2	1	1	1	3	2	1	2	1	2	2	1	2	1	1	1	1	3	1	1	1
	2	2	1	1	2	2	2	3	3	3	3	3	3	3	3	3	2	2	2	1	2	1	3	2	2	1	3	3	2	1	3	2	3	1	2	3	1	2	3	3	3	2	2	3	3
	1	2	1	1	1	1	1	2	2	2	1	1	1	2	3	2	1	1	1	1	1	2	1	1	1	2	1	2	1	2	2	1	2	1	2	3	2	1	2	2
	1	2	1	1	1	1	1	2	2	2	1	1	1	2	2	1	1	1	1	2	1	1	2	2	1	2	2	2	2	1	2	3	3	2	2	2	2
	3	1	3	3	1	3	1	1	1	1	1	1	1	1	1	3	3	1	3	1	3	3	1	1	1	2	1	2	1	2	1	1	1	1	3	1	1	1
	2	1	2	2	1	2	1	1	2	1	1	2	1	1	2	2	2	1	1	2	2	2	1	2	1	1	1	3	1	1	1	1	2	1	1	1
	1	2	1	1	2	1	3	3	3	3	2	2	1	2	2	3	2	1	1	1	2	1	1	2	3	1	1	3	2	2	3	2	1	2	1	1	2	2	3
	2	2	2	2	1	2	1	1	1	1	1	1	1	2	1	1	2	1	1	2	1	1	2	1	1	1	3	1	1	1	1	1	2	3	2	3	2	1	2	1	1	1	2
	1	2	1	1	1	1	1	2	1	1	1	1	1	2	2	1	1	1	1	1	1	2	2	1	2	1	2	1	2	2	1	1	2	1	1	2	2
	2	2	2	2	2	2	2	2	2	2	1	1	2	2	3	2	1	2	1	2	1	1	2	2	1	2	2	2	1	2	2	1	2	2	2	2	2	2	2	2	2
	2	2	2	1	1	1	1	1	1	1	1	1	1	1	1	2	1	1	1	2	1	1	1	1	1	1	3	1	2	1	2	2	2	2	1	1	1	1	1
	1	2	1	1	1	1	1	1	1	1	1	1	1	1	2	1	1	1	1	1	1	2	1	1	2	1	2	1	2	1	1	1	2	1	1	2	3	2
	2	1	2	2	1	1	1	1	1	1	1	1	1	1	1	1	2	2	2	1	2	1	2	2	1	1	2	1	2	2	2	1	1	1	2	1	1	1
	2	2	1	2	2	1	1	2	1	1	1	2	2	2	2	2	1	1	1	1	2	2	1	2	2	1	1	2	1	1	2	1	2	1	2	2
	1	3	1	1	1	1	1	3	3	2	2	2	2	2	2	2	1	1	1	1	1	2	1	2	2	1	1	3	1	2	1	2	1	2	1	1	2	1	2	2	3
	1	2	1	1	2	1	2	3	3	2	3	2	3	2	3	3	2	1	1	1	2	1	3	1	1	2	2	3	1	1	2	1	2	1	2	1	2	1	2	2
	1	2	1	1	2	1	2	3	3	2	3	2	3	3	2	1	2	1	2	1	2	3	2	1	1	3	1	3	2	1	2	1	2	2	1	3	2	2
	3	1	3	3	1	3	1	1	1	1	1	1	1	1	1	1	3	3	1	3	1	3	1	3	3	1	1	3	2	1	2	1	2	2	1	2	1	1	1	1	1	1	1
	2	2	1	1	2	2	3	3	3	2	3	3	3	3	2	2	2	1	2	1	3	1	1	3	3	3	2	1	3	1	3	1	1	3	2	2	2	2	1	1	2	2
	1	1	1	1	2	2	2	1	3	1	1	1	1	2	3	1	1	1	1	2	1	1	2	2	1	1	2	1	2	1	2	1	2	2	1	2	1	2
	1	2	1	1	1	1	1	3	3	2	3	2	2	2	2	2	1	1	1	2	1	1	2	2	2	1	1	2	1	2	1	2	2	1	2	1	3	3	2	2	1	2	2	1

61

Good Display Typography

5

Display type history

GOUDY
FORUM

Based on Roman Architectural Letters

Union Pearl

First Decorative Typestyle

DINNER HORNS

Rimmed Tuscan No. 3

BRINGS CONTENT

Ornamented No. 4

More typestyles than names were
available in the nineteenth century

The first display type was the Roman capital letter. Originally intended for architectural purposes, these letters adorned the sides of buildings and monuments, and were meant to be read from great distances.

The Byzantines were the next to use display type—again as an architectural medium. Large type was part of the mosaic patterns created on the walls and ceilings of their buildings.

The first display type in printed pieces was hand lettering rather than actual fonts of type. Primarily embellishments and initial letters, these were drawn in books after the text had been printed. The artists who drew this early display type were able to keep up with the demand in the fifteenth and sixteenth centuries, when books were still a rare commodity and essentially created by hand. However, as books became available to a wider audience in the seventeenth century, the demand for hand illumination exceeded the ability of artists to create it.

The next logical step was to cast the decorative letters in type. The first of these decorated-display typestyles was Union Pearl. It was initially cast in 1690 by the Stephenson Blake Type Foundry of England, and is still available today in phototype.

The first display typefaces, limited to a few styles, were based primarily on the standard book face designs. They were intended for title pages, chapter headings, and other predominant typography in books. Because of the conservative nature of books, these first display types were conservative in design. Then came the industrial revolution of the nineteenth century and with it advertising. Typography left the bookish confines of publishing to join advertising circles. Many new decorative and novelty display typestyles (often called circus type) were created out of the need to advertise and call attention to manufactured products. By the latter half of the nineteenth century, the demand of advertising and the development of a new, easy method of manufacturing type created a glut of decorated-display typefaces. Manufacturers ran out of fancy names for their typefaces and resorted to calling them "Ornamented No. 4" or "Rimmed Tuscan No. 3."

Also at this time the Art Nouveau influence was beginning to be seen in European typography, and many display typefaces of a different nature were created. Few, however, became popular in America until the Art Nouveau revival of the 1960s.

By the twentieth century most of the overly fancy typestyles had faded from popularity. Advertising, however, was here to stay—and with it the demand for display type. During the first decades of the twentieth century most of the classic display typestyles we are now familiar with were first released: Stymie, Alternate Gothic, Futura, Gill Sans, Goudy Bold and Heavyface, Cooper Black, Standard, Franklin Gothic, Cheltenham, and Clearface, to name a few. It was also at this time that display designs of standard text faces began to appear. This practice continued, so that as new text designs were created, their display counterparts were also released.

Recently, because of the efforts of companies such as International Typeface Corporation (ITC), Type Spectra, and Letraset International Limited, we are witnessing yet another period of prolific display type creation. Although designers and phototype founders haven't yet resorted to numbers instead of names, many compare the current activity in type design with that of the latter part of the last century.

Although the design merits of some new typestyles may be dubious, there has always been, and will probably always be, room to add new designs to the display type spectrum. Communication needs change, typographic styles and fads come and go, and the creative searching of type designers cannot be stifled. An abundance of choice should not be considered a typographic handicap. The best designs always seem to surface to the top anyway. Even during the height of the circus type period, a typeface called French Clarendon Condensed was used far more than any of the other display styles. A hundred years later this typestyle (now known as P. T. Barnum or Playbill) is still in use.

Stymie
Alternate Gothic
Futura
Gill Sans
Goudy Bold
Goudy Heavyface
Cooper Black
Standard
Franklin Gothic
Cheltenham
Clearface

Classic Display Typefaces
All Designed in the Early Twentieth
Century

Playbill

Popular a Hundred Years Ago
and Popular Today

How big?

18 Point Type
48 Point Type

Best Display Size Range

 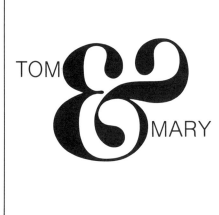

Supersize can be effective.

Display type should have proportional and logical relationships with the other graphic elements on the design surface—even if the only other element is white space.

The best size for display type will naturally vary, depending on typestyle, graphic layout, and other visual elements, but a rule-of-thumb for maximum readability is something between 18 point and 48 point. Larger and smaller sizes can produce excellent results, but there should be a definite reason for using extremely small or large type for display typography.

If utilized carefully, very large display type can be an effective graphic technique. Condensed typestyles, especially sans serif designs, can be used at quite a large size without loss of legibility.

Ideally, copy set in display sizes should be kept to as few words as possible. Long or multiple lines of display typography are not only uninviting, but they are also difficult to read. If long passages of copy are to be set in display sizes, setting them in a condensed typestyle and in lowercase characters will aid in maintaining communication effectiveness and in saving space.

In extremely large sizes, display type assumes a graphic shape as well as letters and words. Creative applications can be quite dynamic: images can be reversed out of the type; other letters and words can be contained within it or be so large that they extend beyond the confines of the design area; single letters or characters of exaggerated size may also serve as a graphic focal point or attention-getter. Oversized display type can create powerful graphics; the key is to maintain legibility of the letterforms and words. *Note*: The technique of using exceptionally large display type is easily overworked.

Display type can also be quite small (only slightly larger than accompanying text composition). If the surrounding white space is utilized effectively and the type does not appear to float in a sea of white space, undersized display typography can create a feeling of dignity or understated elegance. To use small display type correctly requires directly relating it to another graphic element, either to size or placement.

Occasionally blocks of text composition are set in 18-point to 48-point type. Large blocks of display copy handled as text composition can be effective if the right circumstances prevail: if lines of copy are amply leaded, if lines are kept short, and if the typestyle is not too heavy or mono-tone in weight (if the typographic color of the copy is kept light and uncomplicated). This technique can be especially effective if multiple colors or typestyle changes are designed to make the main message emerge from the copy.

While display typography can be pushed to great size extremes and still remain good typography, these design techniques should be handled with care. A good idea is to build a "swipe-file" of especially good display typography. Analyze these pieces to determine why you think they work, and rely on them for guidance in display usage until you feel confident with the medium.

Please Come

We're having a party and we hope you'll come. Now that the summer is drawing to a close, Coleen and I thought it was time to gather the troops together for a final blast. So you bring the beer and we'll provide the crackers, the cheese and other munchies. See you at our house, September 6. It will start at 7 p.m., and go on till the cows come home.

TYPE
A
PREMIER
COLLECTION

Small display type should directly relate to other graphic elements.

The selection of the proper **type** is an important part of the designer's art. **Type** sets the tone for the printed piece. **Type** is the conveyer of mood, it can transport the designer's work into another time and space. **Type** can shout, **type** can whisper, **type** can be the inflection of the spoken word printed on the page. **Type** is the servant of communication. Use **type** to serve you well.

"Message" Within a Message

Uppercase and lowercase display typography

Word shapes aid recognition.

HILLBILLY
hillbilly

COFFEE
coffee

Some words look better set in all capitals, others look better in lowercase.

PHOTOLETTERING
photolettering

Better letterfit is possible with lowercase.

Avoid setting all-capital headlines—it's just that simple.

The objectives of display headlines are to attract the reader's attention, communicate a quick message, and to encourage reading of the accompanying text. All-capital headlines do not adequately meet any of these objectives.

Some background information will make the above statements clearer. Over ninety-five percent of the type we read is lowercase composition. As a result we are much more comfortable reading these characters. Studies also prove that the various heights of different lowercase characters (x-height characters, ascenders, and descenders), when combined to form a word, create an outline shape which is stored in the reader's mind. This word shape then becomes an aid to recognition when the word is seen again. Because of this recall factor, words comprised of lowercase characters can be read much faster than words set in all capitals. All-capital typography creates only a rectangle as a visual identifier.

Lowercase headlines also save space over headlines set in all capitals—up to thirty percent more space. Not only is layout space utilized more efficiently, but fewer movements are made by the eye to perceive the same amount of information.

Lowercase letters, which grew out of the fluidity of handwriting, interrelate better than capital letters. Their shapes are more homogeneous, enabling consistent inter-character spacing relationships. This is true for even reasonably tight letterspacing. Uneven letterspacing is more likely to occur with all-capital typography. The way to correct the spacing problems inherent with all-capital setting is to either letterspace lines of copy to achieve consistent typographic color, or to live with the unevenness. Neither of these is a satisfactory answer by current standards.

One of the few cases when all-capital words can be easier to read than all-lowercase words is when the combination of several similar letter shapes impedes normal reading. The word "hillbilly" is not easily read when set in lowercase. Switching to all capitals remedies this situation. However, the opposite is true in the word "coffee."

When you consider the objectives of a headline, there are only a couple of instances when capitals are more effective than lowercase or capital and lowercase typography: when the lowercase characters are similar in design and may cause reading confusion, or when the combination of capitals is used to create a specific graphic effect or visual pun.

To give importance to a headline, set it in a larger point size or in a bolder typestyle and stay clear of the capital letters; generally they accomplish very little.

LOWERCASE HEADLINES SAVE SPACE

24-Point Type

lowercase headlines save space

24-Point Type

Centering and arrangement of display lines

Typography has always been governed by rules of optics. Because of the increased size, this is especially true of display typography. When working with larger type sizes not only do letterspacing, word spacing, and line spacing have to be considered, but also the centering and alignment of lines.

At 10 point, a forty-five pica line of type is normally perceived as just a line, with no real shape to its terminals. Only when a line of text copy is ended by a punctuation mark do we begin to include optics in line centering and arrangement. However, as point sizes increase the shapes of the letters that begin and end lines become more important.

Correct centering of display lines is rarely a mechanical operation. Over half the lowercase alphabet, and more of the capitals, have shapes which require optical adjustment. Characters such as "A," "T," "V," "X," or "c," "f," "y" create an optical effect whereby the mechanical edge of the letter is different from the perceived edge.

The capital "A" is a perfect example: the mechanical right edge is at that point where the right diagonal meets the baseline; however, the perceived right edge of this character, when centering or aligning lines, is somewhere to the inside of the mechanical edge. When centering or aligning lines of display type, the optical edges of the first and last characters in the line should be considered, not the mechanical. The same holds true for lines beginning or ending with punctuation marks. In many cases the marks must be completely disregarded to attain optical correctness.

A mechanical arrangement of lines, with no regard to character shapes, will almost invariably produce the appearance of uneven alignment. It is when lines are arranged optically (although they may be mechanically uneven), that display typography is at its best.

It has been said, "The eye is the sovereign ruler of taste." This is especially true when working with display type.

**ABCDEFG
JKLOPQRS
TVWXYZ
abcdefgjk
opqrstvwxyz
1234567890**

These are characters that may require special handling when lines are centered.

Mechanical
Edge

Perceived
Edge

Appointment Form
For Typesetting

Mechanical centering produces
an optical imbalance.

Appointment Form
For Typesetting

Optical centering produces an
optical balance.

"Nothing exceeds
like excess."

Centering based
on mechanical edges is poor.

"Nothing exceeds
like excess."

Disregarding punctuation
produces optical centering.

Unique but not overpowering: the best display typestyle

Special Service Tools

Now available.

Our new complete 1979 catalog featuring tools for your VW, Porsche and Audi. Available in both soft and hard cover editions.

Text and display serif typestyles mix well when design differences are obvious.

Strength *Speed*

Avoid the stereotyped in typeface choices.

Probably the best display typestyle is a bold condensed, sans serif design with a large lowercase x-height; its unique design calls attention to itself, yet is easy to read. Certainly you're not going to use the same typestyle for every display application, but if you understand why this design is ideal, it will help you to choose equally good alternatives.

First, if you are mixing text and display typography, the display typestyle should either complement or contrast the text composition. If you are using a serif typeface for text, a display face of sans serif design is a good choice, as is a serif design from the same family, or a bold or bold condensed variant. Mixing faces from the same type family will ensure continuity within the piece you are creating. A serif display typestyle can also be mixed with a different serif text typestyle, but their design differences should be obvious enough to allow distinction for both.

Sans serif designs do not fare quite so well. While they can be contrasted with serif designs, they are not easily complemented by other sans serif typestyles. Most serif-less types share too many similar design traits. *Note*: The Antique Olive family is one exception: it can be mixed quite easily with other sans serif designs.

Usually, display type should be the dominant factor in mixed composition. It should attract attention and entice the reader into the text, but not overpower the text. Although it should be easy to read, display type can afford to be a little uncommon in design. Generally, avoid overly fancy, ornate, or highly stylized display faces.

Condensed typestyles enable more, and larger, characters to be packed into a given area, maximizing the design space. Condensed sans serif designs allow the most compactness without loss of legibility.

Bold designs naturally attract more attention than lighter type weights.

In evocative typography—when you want to create a specific feeling or mood —fancy, overly bold, very light, and "period" designs may become the rule-of-thumb. With this kind of typography two general guidelines should be followed: avoid the obvious and don't be afraid to experiment.

As for the first guideline, we have all seen so much Old English used for antique store ads, and scripts used to promote perfume that their effectiveness in these applications is diminished. Strength does not have to be indicated by a bold sans serif design, and speed is not necessarily best shown through the use of italics. Try to avoid commonplace, obvious typography.

Experiment with evocative typography. "Japanese Cherry Blossoms" can be just as effectively set in a serif typestyle as in a script or mock Oriental typestyle. Keep a swipe-file; as you find typestyles used in unusual or provocative ways, save the samples for future reference.

Make the change
Make the change

Bold typestyles attract attention

space saving space saving
space saving space saving

Condensed typefaces save space.

Overly fancy display typefaces have limited usage.

Japanese Cherry Blossoms   *Japanese Cherry Blossoms*

The obvious is not always the best choice.

Three pitfalls

Since one of the main functions of display typography is to draw attention, more liberties than otherwise acceptable can be taken with the arrangement of words and letters to accomplish this end. Characters can be set tighter than normal to achieve graphic impact, or words can be tilted at an angle to create dynamics and movement. Although it requires skill and sensitivity, letters and words can even be arranged to create visual puns or interesting, eye-catching shapes and patterns.

While opportunities exist for personal expression and graphic experimentation when working with display typography, there are a few graphic techniques that require special care or even avoidance. The irony is that these methods sometimes seem to be the most logical to use.

• Type set in reverse, white type on a dark background, leads the list. The logic behind this technique is that the dark background calls attention to the typography and makes the letters stand out. The problem is that this device may defeat your purpose—because people are less likely to read reverse type. As part of a study to determine typographic readability and legibility standards, it was found that almost eighty percent of the readers preferred black on white typography. And even if the reader's attention could be captured, reverse typography is up to fourteen percent more difficult to read than dark type on a light background.

Reverse type *can* be effective. It should, however, be large in size and limited to just a few words.

• Type should not be set on the vertical, one letter stacked on another. This may be appropriate for café and luncheonette signs where horizontal space is at a premium, but it is not suitable for display typography. In the Western Hemisphere we read on a horizontal axis, and type is designed to work best in this mode. Most people will simply not take the time to try to read a vertical column of display typography. If you must work within a vertical confine, set the type correctly, then place the line on one or the other of its ends.

• Be careful when running type over or through photographs, line art, or illustrations. Within a typographic message the letters and words must be readily discernible and easily read. Other graphic elements mixed with, or overlapping, typography can detract from the communication process. Letters must be the strongest graphic image; if you choose to position type over or near other elements, the typestyle should be sufficiently bold and legible to ensure minimum loss of communication. Avoid fancy, ornate typestyles and scripts.

Although each can be an effective graphic technique under the correct circumstances, reverse type, vertical typesetting, and type overlays should be used with caution.

Vertical typesetting only works for cafés, other businesses, etc.

Here is a possible solution to a vertical confine.

A typographic message must be easily discernible.

connoisseurs' choice

Avoid reverse copy.

Try to keep an open mind.

Visual puns can be effective but are not easy to create.

A Few Hints

Variety and contrast: a simple way to attractive typography

National Old Style This is a design by F. W. Goudy. The contrast of wide and narrow letters makes it similar to his other designs and follows classical precedent.

This head lacks distinction.

National Old Style This is a design by F. W. Goudy. The contrast of wide and narrow letters makes it similar to his other designs and follows classical precedent

Simple changes can add variety.

Typography is more than words on a page—it is language visualized. When the spoken word has vitality, it holds the audience's interest; typography contributes this same vitality to the written word. Through the proper use of variety and contrast, type will attract attention, lend emphasis, and hold the interest of the reader. The pages of type you set or specify need not be dull sheets of monotonous gray texture. With little effort, they can be lively, informative, and inviting.

The easiest way to add variety is to use different sizes of type. An obvious application is contrasting large display headlines with smaller text copy. When used correctly, size variations can also be effective in other situations. For example, in addition to the normal practice of setting running heads in a bold face, the point size of these heads can also be increased. In extended text settings, applying the newspaper method of shading down—setting the opening line or two in a large text point size, the succeeding paragraph in a point size smaller, and the remainder of the copy in a third smaller point size—often makes lengthy copy look more inviting. Take care not to use a poin size too small for body copy (8 point should be the minimum).

Although size changes can add strength to the printed piece, too many variations create confusion. For this reason, type sizes should only be changed when it helps to convey the intended message. Two sizes can enliven a short page while three sizes are usually sufficient to improve an average-size page of complicated text settings.

Contrast through type-size variation is best illustrated by the accompanying advertisement. Because it was set in the same point size, the first example lacks contrast and emphasis.

This ad needn't be dull, however, even though it uses only a small group of type. Note how in the resetting the feature line has been stressed by increasing the point size. Since the second and third lines require less emphasis, their point size has been decreased giving more notability to the first line. Prominence is also given to the company name through use of a third point size.

The contrast of bold and light typefaces also adds distinction. The weight of type used for headings should normally be heavier than type used for body copy. This is especially true if headlines are set in a different typeface. Compare the following two examples. In the first, even though the head is set in a larger size, it lacks distinction.

Simply changing from a medium to bold weight corrects this problem.

Another area where the use of bold type can be applied is when words of particular importance within text copy are set in boldface for emphasis. This can build an inviting texture on the page and create several mini-headlines within the copy. Tabular work can be made easier to read by the systematic use of bold type to aid the eye in distinguishing sets of information. Changes in typestyles can also add energy and life, and the use of novelty faces can evoke a specific feeling. The example not only contains the pertinent information concerning the rodeo, it also conveys a western feeling.

Varying line lengths in display work can be just as important as changing type styles or sizes. An otherwise dull piece of typography can be enriched through simple variation of line lengths. By shortening the second and fourth lines, this ad takes on a new life with added emphasis in areas that deserve it.

In some instances, one long line may be broken into two shorter lines of varying lengths to achieve a dynamic effect. Care must be taken, however, to break the line at a logical place; otherwise, the copy can become confusing. By resetting with a logical break in the line the message is clear and strong.

When trying to enliven your typography through contrast and variety, it is important to realize that these elements are built on easily identifiable differences. If the differences between the typographic elements are too subtle, little is accomplished. The other side of the coin is that, although contrast and variety can make typeset copy more interesting, moderation should be used to ensure that it remains easily readable. Too much variety is not pleasing to the eye and also creates confusion, as shown in the example.

Discretion is the key to contrasting and varying typographic elements that will generate interest, emphasis, and above all vitality.

3RD ANNUAL
BANGOR RODEO
SATURDAY JULY 4
BANGOR FAIRGROUNDS

Western Type, Western Feeling

Punch somebody in Texas with the General Telephone push-button phone.

Confusing headlines can be caused by poor line breaks.

Punch somebody in Texas with the General Telephone push-button phone.

The better the line break, the better the typography.

Dot La Pas

School of Charm and Modeling

Personal Improvement & Professional Modeling

Etiquette * Poise * Posture

Personal Interview Arranged

Call 555-1212

Too much variety can be just as bad as too little.

STEREO EQUIPMENT
Largest Selection in New England
Satisfaction Guaranteed
Boston Stereo Company
Boston, Mass.

Boring

STEREO EQUIPMENT
Largest Selection in New England
Satisfaction Guaranteed
Boston Stereo Company
Boston, Mass.

Eye-Catching

FUNCTION HALLS
Weddings • Banquets • Receptions
Elegantly Decorated Function Rooms
Ultimate in Taste and Perfection
The Hillcrest Plaza

Several lines close to the same length can be dull.

FUNCTION HALLS
Weddings • Banquets • Receptions
Elegantly Decorated Function rooms
Ultimate in Taste and Perfection
The Hillcrest Plaza

Varying line lengths can help typography.

Initial letters

 aste in printing will determine the form typography shall take. The selection of a congruous typeface, the quality and suitability for its purpose of the paper to be used, and the care and labor, time and cost of materials all in a direct ratio to its worth and destiny.

Fancy Initial

By the time the job is ready for printing, it has gone through many hands, each contributing its own individual expertise to produce a small masterpiece. No one person can truly receive full credit for the finished product.

Upsized Character
of Same Typeface

Initial letters can be of many styles and used in several ways. Some are quite fancy and obviously different from standard capital letters, while others are nothing more than up-sized standard characters.

Initials are used to mark the beginning of book chapters, as eye-catching ornaments in display typography or advertising pieces, for reference guides in continuous text composition, and, in some cases, for setting headlines.

The most common usage, as an ornamental mark at the start of a paragraph, is generally handled in one of two ways: as a dropped initial or as a raised initial. Both will add variety to your typography.

A dropped initial should meet the following criteria: the top of the initial should align optically with the top of the text composition. Round letterforms, or characters with a pointed apex, will align slightly higher than the mathematical top to appear correct. The bottom of the initial should, when possible, align with the baseline of the second, or a succeeding, line of text. The left ends of lines indented to accommodate the initial should fit closely to the right edge of the initial, either justified flush left, or following the contour of the initial. The left side of the initial should optically align with the left edge of the body of text composition.

Raised initials follow the same criteria except they extend above the first line of copy, and must always align with the baseline of a line of text.

Initials Used as Headlines

Although there is no apparent assembly line in typesetting, the job moves from operation to operation to its completion.

Book Chapter Opening

A As typesetting jobs move from step to step, they're often accompanied by the ever present query, "What do you want me to do with this?"

B Between the time a job enters the premises and the time someone begins to apply productive hours to it, a very important function must take place—planning and analysis. You may also call this scheduling.

C One of the most vital functions in an automated composition facility is that of job entry and mark-up.

Reference Guides

Even though there is no apparent assembly line in the typesetting process, there is still the movement of the job from operation to operation.

As typesetting jobs move from step to step they are usually accompanied by the ever-present query, "What would you like me to do with this thing?"

One of the most important functions in any automated composition facility is that of job entry and rough layouts.

Correct Placement of
Dropped Initials

Typo Graphic Design

Ornaments

Even though there is no apparent assembly line in the typesetting process, there is still the movement of the job from operation to operation.

Correct Placement of
Raised Initial

Typesetting is a cumulative process. From the time a job enters the production operation until it exits in finished form, many people and many steps complete the finished product through successive additions.

Dropped Initial

Typesetting is a cumulative process. From the time a job enters the production operation until it exits in finished form, many people and many steps complete the finished product through successive additions.

Raised Initial

Tight isn't necessarily right

Graphic impact created
by tight typography.

Legibility

Too tight spacing causes
poor letter combinations.

Legibility

Even spacing creates
readability.

We are firmly entrenched in phototype technology. The first generation of photo-typesetting technology has been fully replaced by the second generation, which began life in the early 1950s. Digitized fonts (type designs held in electronic memory) and laser imaging are not only in use today, but promise to soon become the industry standard. With this new technology has come typographic freedom. Today, typography has more flexibility and is bound by fewer constraints than has ever been possible outside of hand lettering or calligraphy.

At the center of all this typographic freedom is the ability to control the proportions of interletter spacing. We tend to be influenced, when we specify and set type, by what many call a "new sense of legibility." We are not only told that tight letterspacing is better typography and more effective communication, but also that it is aesthetically pleasing. True statements? Maybe. However, first it is worthwhile to look back to see how we arrived at the point where tight letterspacing is so popular.

At the same time Gutenberg freed the scribes from being the sole source of graphic communication, he also imposed technological restrictions on graphic design. No longer was graphic communication to be a delicate and sensitive letter-by-letter rendering.

Each letter was cast in a block of metal, and bound by the physical restrictions of that block. Therefore, in most handset composition there was no such thing as "tight type" or letterspace compensation.

When typesetting technology advanced to metal type set by machine, individual letter kerning and other typographic refinements suffered even more. Composing machines provided more speed, but with speed came standardization. Many fonts were "duplexed" to save costs and gain efficiency; when the various weights of a typeface were engineered to occupy the same space or unit value, many times the resultant design created poor typography.

Display typesetting did fare a little better. Since display type is by nature larger in size, it was easier to trim or adjust the spacing dictated by the metal slugs.

The first phototypesetters were patterned primarily after existing metal type technology. Few offered the sophistication of kerning and compensation. Although tight letterspacing could be achieved with some machines, not many typographers attempted it, and if they did, the results were usually poor.

Within a few years, all levels of photo-typesetting equipment incorporated typographic refinements. Along with this, the ability to compensate letterspacing became commonplace. In the hands of a good operator, these machines were capable of producing subtle spacing of characters. Few still attempted experimentation with tightly set text type until the use of visually spaced photo display typesetters became popular. With these machines, tight headlines became the order of the day (and were considered good graphics). Because of the success with display type, graphic designers and advertising typographers began to experiment with tight text typesetting.

Compensation programs within text typesetters were, by this time, refined and the results predictable. Tight text type began to be specified regularly, and the industry began to talk of a new legibility.

For those who would believe that tight letterspacing aids readability, creates effective communication, and is aesthetically pleasing, there is some good news—and some bad.

First the good news. Yes, there are definite advantages to tight letterspacing, especially in display typography. It can create graphic illustrations in which the letters become more than simple representations of sounds. Tight letterspacing can also pack more words into a given line measure and save space. If handled carefully and with skill, tightly set display type can create strength and impact in headlines.

Now, the bad news. The result of tight letterspacing is only as good as the type-setter or specifier responsible for the job. It takes a sensitive and highly trained eye to set tight display type. Someone with the experience and ability to correctly set, interlock, and interweave characters can create a pleasing graphic form as illustrated. It is too easy, however, for someone inexperienced or uncomfortable with type to create a graphic "blob."

Then there is always the language barrier between the type specifier and the person setting the type. What one considers to be good typography the other may not. "How tight is tight?" is still the nagging issue between the person ordering and those setting type. The poor letter combination that throws off a complete line of tightly set type must also be contended with. (The solution is to reset the line so that it is not so tight.)

Note in the first example how poor letter combinations call attention to themselves. The reader sees these and the effectiveness of the headline is lost. A little more space between the letters, as in the second example, reduces the risk of losing the reader's attention.

In addition, many typefaces, no matter how carefully they are set, are simply not conducive to tight display typesetting. The illustration is an example of such a face. It would be very difficult, if not impossible, to create effective communication using this typeface set tightly. An interesting graphic form may be created, but that is not enough to qualify as good typography. Faces to be avoided when setting tight type are: those with large full serifs as in the LSC Book, Tiffany, or Clarendon families; typefaces that have strong thick and thin contrasts such as Bodoni or Didi, and typefaces like Eurostile and Gill Ultrabold that are extended in design or have large, open counters.

Headlines are normally read at a glance, and, therefore, must be absolutely readable. If overly tight letterspacing in a headline causes the least confusion in letterform definition, the reader will not spend the time to decipher the meaning.

The point at which "tight" becomes "overly tight" arrives much sooner when setting text copy. This is because a text typeface design is created out of the space between letters as much as the letters themselves. These positive and negative spaces create a texture that tight letterspacing can, and often does, destroy. The largest percentage of all text faces used today were not designed to be set tight.

Insistence on doing so will not only degrade the original design, but will also seriously inhibit the communicative power of the typeface. The spotty areas of heavy texture where letters come very close, or touch, can tire the eye and make reading a slow, difficult process. These areas may also cause the eye to stop in places where it is not logical to do so; or to jump from one black spot to another, breaking the sentence structure.

Overlapping the touching characters can also create shapes unfamiliar to the eye, causing the reader to stop momentarily in order to logically sort them out.

Usually, only when text copy is set in large sizes (14 point or larger) can tight letterspacing become an effective typographic tool.

There are several familiar, contemporary text faces specifically designed for tight letterspacing, but even these should be used with care.

Is tight right? In specific situations and when handled cautiously the answer is yes. For the greater percentage of graphic communication, however, the answer must be no.

Avant Garde Gothic
Antique Olive
Serif Gothic
ITC Souvenir

These can be set tight easily.

LSC Book
Bodoni
Didi
Eurostile
Gill Ultrabold

Avoid setting too tight.

One typeface can differ from another in various ways. Some design characterics to look for are: the relationship between the lowercase x-height and the capital letters; also it should be

Tight letterspacing and
loose word spacing
decrease legibility.

Diversification: a way to increase profits

COPPERPLATE LIGHT CONDENSED

COPPERPLATE LIGHT

COPPERPLATE HEAVY

Some of the Copperplate Family

Diversification into other areas of typesetting is a natural, yet often overlooked, way to improve profits. This is not to say that you should go into competition with large specialty printers and typesetters, but the opportunity exists to satisfy typesetting needs of customers who do not require the expertise of these specialty houses. For example, the special interest groups, ethnic organizations, small companies, or individuals with particular typesetting requirements are all candidates to be new customers for you. Many times their requirements are no more demanding than good typography using a specialized typeface or complement of characters.

If their type needs are now being satisfied by typewriters, dry-transfer lettering, or not at all, the majority of these people would welcome the opportunity to have their material typeset. By providing this service you will be upgrading the typographic quality of their printed pieces and increasing your profit margin. Consider the following typefaces and character complements—can you put them to good use?

Copperplate Family

Copperplate is invaluable for setting business cards, letterheads, and professional or official forms. Nearly eighty percent of all work of this nature uses the Copperplate typestyle. It is capable of setting very small sizes (the equivalent of 3½-point type) while still being highly readable.

Invitations or Social Scripts

Social announcements, bar mitzvah invitations, and fine social stationery are usually typeset and printed by large specialty houses. However, with script typefaces you could be servicing the social printing needs in your area. Although much of this work is done with raised lettering, beautiful and effective announcement printing can be achieved without the aid of engraving or thermography.

Greek and Math

Greek and math fonts are available for most phototypesetters manufactured. While some math typesetting is extremely difficult and can only be performed by highly trained typographers using very costly typesetting equipment, there is a great deal of math typesetting that is relatively simple to set and can be easily handled by basic Greek and math fonts. There are books available to guide the novice in basic math typesetting. One of the best I have seen is published by the National Composition Association, and is available from them for approximately twenty dollars. It is important to realize that a large portion of most typesetting involving Greek and math is the text copy, not the equations. Therefore, if you can offer simple math typesetting capabilities, you may be able to attract large jobs of text composition.

Multilingual

By using a multilingual character complement, you can turn your typesetter into a machine capable of setting many languages. Numerous ethnic groups have cultural and social societies that publish small newsletters or announcements. In many cases these publications are being set on a typewriter with accents and/or non-English characters drawn by hand. With a multilingual or language filmstrip, you could aid these groups with their typesetting needs. *Note*: To avoid problems you should either have a good working knowledge of the language or have access to a good translator, since setting a foreign language can be somewhat confusing at first.

Condensed Typefaces

Every business, large or small, has a need for forms of one kind or another. Most small companies buy their forms from large printers or supply houses that offer a standard format. However, adding several condensed faces in text sizes will enable you to offer the service of custom-tailored forms to small business in your area.

Swash Typefaces, Borders, Symbols, and Initials

Tasteful use of these elements can add beauty and effectiveness to the ads you print. By showing variety in your work, you can attract new advertising business. Be sure to use these elements with discretion since too much variety can cause confusion and result in ineffectual typography.

Social Scripts	*Flemish Script Venetian Script Riviera Script Florentine Script Stuyvesant Engravers Text Floridian Script French Script Piranesi Italic Park Avenue Liberty*

Greek and Math

ΑΒΓΔΕΖΗΘΙΚΛΜΝΞΟΠΡΣΤΥΦΧΨΩ αβγδεζηϑικλμνξοπςϱστ υφχψω ∵∴∷÷≐̄ ̱ ̄ ̠–=̇+̄−±∓×ˣ∦≢≠∓≅≃☉☺∅♂♀®©@ ○°𝔛 1234567890 1234567890 ʺʹ ˎˎ ∵☉α∞∞∼≈∫φ§∿⟩⟨√ †‡R$£#{} ⁰₍₁[]⁽⁾₍₎()◊≫≪≥≶≷≥⟩⟨∠▷◀△▽ᐃ△π∕∖∥∣∕⊥∣∕∕↔↕↑↓→←↱ ↰∧∴↕⇌⇋☐⌈⌐⌊⌋⊏⊃⊂◌∵∴ ΑΒΓΔΕΖΗΘΙΚΛΜΝΞΟΠΡΣΤΥ ΦΧΨΩ αβγδεζβϑικλμνξοπςϱστυφχψω ∵∴∷÷≐̄ ̱ ̄ ̠–=̇+̄− ∓×ˣ∦≢≡+≅≃☉☺∅♂♀®©@○°𝔛 1234567890 1234567890 ʺʹ ˎˎ ☉α

Multilingual

ABCDEFGHIJKLMNOPQRSTUVWXYZ&
abcdefghijklmnopqrstuvwxyz
ÇÑçéıñß ̈ ̂ ̀ ́ (.,:; * / - - — . _ _ ¿?¡!«»)
1234567890%¢$/£°†® © • ● ✔ @ □ º ª = + ÷

Condensed Typefaces

TASTE IN PRINTING DETERMINES THE FORM TYPOGRAPHY IS
TASTE IN PRINTING DETERMINES THE FORM TYPOGRAPHY
TASTE IN PRINTING DETERMINES THE FORM TYPOGRAPHY IS TO
TASTE IN PRINTING DETERMINES THE FORM TYPOGR

Swash, Borders, Symbols

ABCGKNOSTThYMR&fKmn o rvwye

Familiar Faces

7

The basic faces you should know

There is a theory in art that says you cannot draw something you do not know. This is one of the reasons drawing students study anatomy; the workings of the human body must be understood before they can be rendered properly.

The same theory has validity in typography. The more you know about a typeface, the easier it will be for you to use it properly. In addition, it's fun to know a little history and background of the tools of the typographic trade—typefaces.

What follows is a series of short chapters to acquaint you with the typefaces you should know:

Antique Olive

There is a theory that current sans serif typeface designs evolved from the square- or slab-serifed styles popular in the last century. These heavy designs were used in advertising to attract the reader's attention. As new typestyles were designed increasingly bolder, it became difficult to incorporate serifs into the designs, and as a result serifs were shortened. This tendency, together with the demand for new alphabets, contributed to the emergence of sans serif typestyles.

Antique Olive is a natural evolution from earlier nineteenth-century typestyles. Designed in the mid-1960s by Roger Excoffon, Antique Olive is one of the more versatile sans serif typestyles. An exceptionally large lowercase x-height and unique weight stress at the tops of characters also make Antique Olive strikingly different from most sans serif designs.

Lowercase characters are slightly condensed and have very short ascenders and descenders. Curved shapes are somewhat squared and the terminals of open characters are clipped. The dots over the "i" and "j" are flattened, the top-heavy weight stress makes the "s" appear upside down, and the terminal of the "e" almost touches the cross bar.

In the capitals, the terminal and stem of the "G" almost touch, and the diagonals of the "K" meet at the stem. Because they are the same length, the middle arms of the "E" and "F" appear longer than their counterparts.

The large lowercase x-height and condensed character proportions give display sizes of Antique Olive strong visibility and make it an effective user of space. However, lines of text do need a little additional line space for maximum readability. An added benefit of Antique Olive is that it is one of the few sans serif designs that mixes well with other sans serif typefaces.

Nineteenth-Century Square-Serif Designs

Unique

Antique Olive's Large x-Height and
Unique Weight Stress to Characters

optic

Slightly Condensed,
Somewhat Squared Round Characters
Clipped Terminals

ij

Flattened Dots

s

Appears Upside Down

G

Terminal and Stem
Almost Touching

K

Diagonals Meeting
at Stem

e

Terminal almost
touches cross bar.

EF

Middle arms
appear long.

ITC Avant Garde Gothic

ITC Avant Garde Gothic Oblique

ITC Lubalin Graph

a   s

One-Storied "a"   Condensed "s"

ABCDEFGHIJKLMNOPQRSTUVWXYZ
abcdefghijklmnopqrstuvwxyz

Narrow Caps Compared with Lowercase Letters

A AC CA EA FA R GA CE
TH HT LA LA LM NT
R KA RA SS ST ST UT V VW
e tv w y œ œ
ff fi ffi fl ffl

Alternate Characters and Special Ligatures

ITC Avant Garde Gothic

ITC Avant Garde Gothic was originally created in 1962 as the logo typeface for *Avant-Garde* magazine. Herb Lubalin, then the magazine's art director and originator of the type design, was asked on many occasions to add more weights to the original design and release it for general use. He declined until 1970, when ITC (International Typeface Corporation) was formed. The five basic weights of ITC Avant Garde Gothic family—extralight, book, medium, demi, and bold— were then made available as part of ITC's initial typeface release program. Since then four condensed designs, five designs with slab serifs (known as ITC Lubalin Graph), and ITC Avant Garde Gothic Oblique (a group of five italics) have been added to the original series.

The ITC Avant Garde Gothic family is easily recognizable by its unusually large lowercase x-height. The family is proportionally larger than most sans serif faces; it is larger than Univers and much larger than Futura, with which it shares many design traits.

The lowercase "a" is one-storied, the lowercase "s" quite condensed, and the capitals are narrow in comparison to the full-bodied lowercase.

The ITC Avant Garde Gothic family is appropriate for typesetting applications that call for a distinctive, modern design. The light weights look best in text copy and only the display designs have the alternate characters and special ligatures. *Note*: Long blocks of text copy should be amply leaded for maximum readability.

The next time you are working with copy that only fills one-half or three-quarters of a page, try setting it in 14- or 18-point ITC Avant Garde Gothic Book. It will fill the page and create a strong graphic effect.

Baskerville

Baskerville is probably the most popular serif typeface in the world. It is a part of every phototype manufacturer's type library and is used for every typesetting application you can imagine. In Japan, for instance, Baskerville appears to be the most extensively used Latin alphabet. This is an interesting coincidence since historians attribute the sale and trade of Japanese ware as the reason for the wealth of John Baskerville, the typeface's designer.

Baskerville has not always been this popular. Designed in the 1750s and primarily used for private press work, it was not seen much by the general public for its first twenty-five years. After John Baskerville's death, the designs were sold to a French foundry. For the next twenty years Baskerville was used only sporadically in Europe, and by the late 1700s the designs were lost to the public eye. Baskerville's revival is credited to the 1923 version released by the Monotype Corporation.

Baskerville is considered a transitional typeface. It contains characteristics found in both oldstyle designs, such as Bembo or Garamond, and in modern type designs, such as Bodoni and Didot. The oldstyle characteristics are especially apparent in the bracketed serifs of the lowercase "i," "k," and "m," while modern typestyle traits are found in the vertical weight stress of the character strokes. In comparison to other typefaces, Baskerville has large and full-bodied lowercase proportions. It is said that publishers wishing to add length and importance to short manuscripts would set them in Baskerville because it took up space.

The best interpretations of Baskerville have strong weight contrasts between the thick and thin stresses with carefully drawn transitions. This design is readily recognized by the open bowl of the lowercase "g," the projecting lower arm of the capital "E," and the spur serif on the capital "G."

Baskerville, a formal alternative to Times Roman, can be used for almost all typesetting applications, except where space is at a premium. Its design characteristics make it an extremely legible typeface well suited to extended text settings. The Baskerville family is a most valuable addition to all commercial type libraries.

ikm

Bracketed Serifs

CcDd

Vertical Weight Stress

ABCDEFGHIJKLMNOPQRSTUVWXYZ
abcdefghijklmnopqrstuvwxyz

Garamond—An Oldstyle Design

ABCDEFGHIJKLMNOPQRSTUVWXYZ
abcdefghijklmnopqrstuvwxyz

Baskerville—A Transitional Design

ABCDEFGHIJKLMNOPQRSTUVWXYZ
abcdefghijklmnopqrstuvwxyz

Bodoni—A Modern Design

abcdefghijklmnopqrstuvwxyz

Large Lowercase Proportions of Baskerville

abcdefghijklmnopqrstuvwxyz

Set in Bembo at the Same Point Size

E   G

Long   Spur
Lower   Serif
Arm

g

Open
Loop

Hbap

Condensed Characters and Short x-Height
Long Ascenders and Descenders

KmnE

Curved Strokes on ''K'' ''m'' ''n''
Nearly Equal-Length Top and Middle Arms of ''E''

aTe

Small Bowl of ''a''
Wide ''T''
High Cross Bar of ''e''

Bembo

Many regard Bembo as the most beautiful oldstyle type design. It is based on a manuscript typeface first used in 1495. The modern revival of this classic derives its name from the manuscript's writer, Pietro Bembo, rather than the type designer. One manufacturer does give credit to the designer, Francesco Griffo, by naming their version of this type family Griffo.

The typefaces now classified as oldstyle dominated most European printing until the end of the seventeenth century. All of these faces were derived from the designs created by Griffo. The early French type designers used Griffo's designs as a model to produce faces such as Garamond. Dutch type designers copied the French, and the British based their work on the Dutch designs. Therefore, from the work of Claude Garamond to modern revivals such as Palatino, the heritage of these designs can be traced to the original Bembo of 1495.

The current Bembo design is an excellent text typestyle. Its qualities of being somewhat condensed and having a small lowercase x-height make it a good choice when saving space is a major concern. The ascenders and descenders are long, giving the design a feeling of grace while retaining a high level of readability and legibility, even when set solid, that is, with no additional line space.

Bembo is easily identified by the curved diagonals of the capital ''K,'' the curve to the final vertical strokes of the lowercase ''m'' and ''n,'' and the nearly equal length of the top and middle arms of the capital ''E.'' Other distinguishing characteristics include a wide capital ''T,'' the small bowl on the lowercase ''a,'' and high cross bar on the lowercase ''e.'' The lowercase ascenders are also taller than the capitals.

Bembo's light weight, delicate serifs, and small counters create beautiful text composition. These same features, however, dictate careful handling when working in small point sizes or on a coarse paper stock.

Bodoni

Using the term "modern" to classify a typestyle of the seventeenth century puzzled me for a long time. Finally, I learned that the term was coined over a hundred years ago to describe those type designs created as new alternatives to the calligraphic oldstyle designs of the period. Bembo is a classic example of an oldstyle type design; Bodoni is the archetypal modern typestyle.

In the early twentieth century use of these modern designs saw a revival. It was then that Morris Benton created his type design based on the work of Giambattista Bodoni, one of the seventeenth-century masters of the modern style.

The design traits of Bodoni are directly attributed to the technological advancements in printing techniques of the time. The quality of paper stock had improved so that the fine character definition of this typeface was possible. In addition, copperplate engraving became a popular printing technique, enabling reproduction of very fine lines.

The chief characteristics of Bodoni are extremely fine hairlines and thick stems. The ascenders and descenders are also normally very long. The round letters tend to be condensed, with almost mathematical vertical stress. The serifs of this typeface are thin, flat, and unbracketed.

Bodoni is an easy typestyle to spot, but characters that help to identify it are the capital "C," which has serifs at both top and bottom, the condensed capital "M," and the capital "Q," which has a vertical tail. The lowercase "g" has a small upper bowl, the lowercase "w" has no middle serif, and the "c" has a large ball terminal.

Bodoni is not a particularly good typestyle to use for extended text composition. The extreme contrast of weights creates the optical effect called "dazzling," which makes reading difficult. The book weight works fairly well in long blocks of text copy, but it should be used judiciously. Because of its contrast in weight and condensed design, Bodoni was used extensively for newspaper headlines until recently. A strong graphic effect can be created when using Bodoni for display headlines, but it, too, should be handled with discretion. Although Bodoni is one of the most distinctive typestyles available to the typographer, it is also one of the most difficult to use effectively.

Bodo

Sharp Hairlines, Thick Stems
Condensed Rounds with Vertical Stress

Unbracketed Serif

ABCDEFGHIJKLMNOPQRSTUVWXYZ
abcdefghijklmnopqrstuvwxyz

Bembo—The Classic Oldstyle

ABCDEFGHIJKLMNOPQRSTUVWXYZ
abcdefghijklmnopqrstuvwxyz

Bodoni—The Archetype Modern

CMQ

Top and Bottom Serifs on "C"
Condensed "M"
Vertical Tail of "Q"

gwc

Small Bowl of "g"
No Middle Serif on "w"
Large Ball Terminal of "c"

Bangle

Monotone Weight
Strong Serifs
Large x-Height

T

Top Serifs Splayed

mn

Inclined Roman Rather Than Cursive Design

B R P

Flat Bowls

g

Ear emits from center of bowl.

E F

Long Arms

Q &

Fancy Designs

a

Two Storied
Flat Bowl

g

Bottom Loop
Flat

m n u

Angled Head-Serifs and Flat Shoulders

S

Snake-Like Appearance

Bookman

Bookman has been around and popular since the 1890s. Its design is based on another popular typeface called Oldstyle Antique, which became available in the 1850s. Oldstyle Antique was in such demand that most type founders designed their own versions of it. When American Type Founders merged with several foundries in the late 1800s, they acquired various designs of this typestyle. Only one was released—under the name Bookman.

Bookman is almost monotone in weight, with strong serifs and a large lowercase x-height. In the capitals, the bowls of the "B," "P," and "R" are flat, the top serifs of the "T" are splayed, and the arms of the "E" and "F" are long. An easy character to remember is the "S": it's been described as looking like a snake ready to strike.

In the lowercase the head serifs are angled. The "a" is the usual two-storied design and has a flat bowl; the bottom loop of the "g" is also flat. The "m," "n," and "u" have flat shoulders, not a smooth curve.

Bookman Italic is an inclined roman, rather than a cursive design. The "Q" and ampersand are quite fancy, and the ear of the "g" emits from the center of the bowl.

Over the years a variety of swash characters have been designed for Bookman; recently, International Typeface Corporation released an updated design of the family.

Bookman is ideally suited to display applications and short blocks of text composition. It is a strong, straightforward typestyle that can create beautiful and distinctive display typography through the use of its swash characters.

Century Old Style

Century Old Style is based on the original type designs of Linn Boyd Benton for *Century* magazine. Designed by his son, Morris Benton, in 1906, as part of the growing Century family, Century Old Style was (until recently) overshadowed by both Century Schoolbook and Century Expanded. The first Century design was intended to be more readable than previous typestyles; Century Old Style is a natural outgrowth of that first typeface.

Although similar to other faces in the Century family, Century Old Style is easily distinguished by the large angled serifs on the top of the capitals "F," "G," and "T." This angular serif design is also repeated on the bottom of the capitals "E" and "S." The apex of the capital "A" is angled slightly and the capital "G" has just a hint of a spur. The lowercase letters are slightly condensed and almost vertical in weight stress, while the lowercase "g" is somewhat unusual in that the top and bottom bowl do not appear to match.

In text composition, the serifs are long and can easily touch if the copy is set too tightly.

Century Old Style, although not particularly eloquent or fancy, is truly an American masterpiece. A very practical typeface, it is both highly readable and legible, even under less-than-perfect printing conditions. It works equally well for both text and display applications, but its real strength lies in setting lengthy blocks of text composition. Century Old Style has always been one of my favorites.

FGTES
Wide-Angled Serifs

A G
Angled   Slight
Apex   Spur

g
Very Unmatched Bowl and Loop

Hillbilly
Long Serifs

News Gothic

Alternate Gothic

Franklin Gothic

Designed Prior to Futura

Uu

Cap and Lowercase "u":
Same Design

ij

Round dots on "i" and "j"
The "j" has straight stem.

One-Storied "a"

Futurax**xAntique Olive**

Futura

Although Futura was not the first sans serif design used in the United States, it has to be considered a classic example of that typestyle. News Gothic, Alternate Gothic, and Franklin Gothic were all released prior to Futura, but Futura has the credit of popularizing the sans serif design. Released in 1927 by Bauer Type Foundry of Germany, the original concepts of Futura are based on the design philosophy that "form follows function." Futura is a type design stripped to the bare essentials. It contains no "frills," such as serifs, and has no weight stresses, or curves, unless they are absolutely necessary.

The single character that most easily identifies Futura is the one-storied lowercase "a" (like the kind we were taught to print in grade school). Other distinguishing characteristics of this typeface are the straight-stemmed lowercase "j," the lowercase "u," which shares the same design as the capital, and the round dots over the lowercase "i" and "j."

Futura has a comparatively small x-height for a sans serif face. This enables it to be set with slightly less line space and more characters in a given area than other popular sans serif designs. A drawback is that the lowercase appears small and does not carry the visual impact of other sans serif designs with a larger x-height.

Futura can be used for almost all typesetting applications; however, its monotone weight detracts from reading ease in extended text settings (the eye seems to need slight weight changes in character strokes to relieve reading fatigue). The bold weights are used extensively in advertising headlines. The bold and extra-bold weights add authority to this family that already communicates objectivity and directness.

Garamond

The first designer and founder to produce type specifically for retail was Claude Garamond. Until he began this practice in Paris early in the sixteenth century, printers had to cast their own type. It is only fitting that this pioneer of typography be remembered by an elegant and popular typestyle bearing his name.

Garamond is one of the most venerable typestyles in current use; the original cuts date back to the sixteenth century. Classified as a "French Oldstyle" design, Garamond is one of the most graceful and refined text types.

The general appearance of Garamond is marked by the subtle weight changes, a small lowercase x-height, and long ascenders and descenders. The capital "T" has one of the most famous trademarks in type—the top left serif slants, while the right serif is straight. Other identifiers of the Garamond typeface include the high cross bar on the capital "A" and the overlapping inner strokes of the capital "W." The counters of the lowercase "a" and "e" are considered very small while the "c" has a wide opening.

In text composition, Garamond conserves space in two ways: the small x-height allows more words to be set in a given area, and the long ascenders and descenders make it one of the few typefaces that can be set solid (no additional line space).

Note: When setting small point sizes (8 point or less) or printing on an inexpensive stock, take care that the small lowercase counters do not fill in—something that can happen easily. All other times, you can't go wrong using Garamond.

abcdefghijklmnopqrstuvwxyz

Subtle Weight Changes
Small x-Height
Long Ascenders and Descenders

T

The left serif slants, the
right serif is straight.

A

High
Cross Bar

ae

Small Closed
Counters

W

Strokes
overlap.

c

Open counter has
wide opening

agt

Based on Serif Designs

M

Diagonals descend only halfway.

abcdefghijklmnopqrstuvwxyz

14-Point Gill Sans

abcdefghijklmnopqrstuvwxyz

14-Point Helvetica

Live Life!

Gill Ultrabold

Gill Sans

Gill Sans is the British counterpart to Futura. In 1927, Monotype Corporation commissioned Eric Gill to create a type-style, with the purpose of diverting the flood of sans serif designs coming out of German foundries as a result of the immediate success of Futura. Although legend has it that the design for Gill Sans is derived from a typeface used by the London Underground Railroad, Eric Gill felt he owed little to that influence. Eric Gill is regarded as one of the pioneers of contemporary typography and can be considered a modern Renaissance man. He was a writer, a sculptor, a stonecutter, an artist, and a graphic designer. (Included among his friends were Bertrand Russell, Henry James, and Virginia Woolf.)

In contrast to Futura and other similar faces, Gill is not based on geometric shapes. Most of the characters are derived from classical serif designs. Perhaps it is this feature that entitles Gill Sans to be termed the most readable and legible sans serif typeface.

The lowercase "a," "g," and "t" are the most easily recognizable serif-based designs.

The lowercase x-height of Gill Sans is considered small by current standards, and the counters do not have the even, round shapes found in most sans serif designs.

The capitals are uniform in width and the diagonals of the cap "M" only descend halfway.

Gill Sans is currently popular for advertising. The lighter weights are used for body copy and the bolds for headlines. Gill Ultrabold, or Kayo, is an especially effective attention-getter.

A clean, functional appearance and high legibility/readability factors make Gill a natural for setting extended text copy, or for use anytime reading ease is of prime importance.

Goudy Old Style

Goudy Old Style has been popular since it was first released in 1915. Today, it numbers among the favorites of advertising designers and typographers. Like many other designs by Frederic Goudy, Goudy Old Style is based on the early work of Italian type designers. The diagonal stress of the character weights is the most obvious trait of these early Italian, or Venetian oldstyle, type designs. The descenders in Goudy Old Style are somewhat short in comparison with the other classic oldstyle faces, and Frederic Goudy felt this was a design flaw on his part. Ironically, short descenders and ascenders are now popular in type design.

There are many other distinguishing characteristics of the Goudy Old Style family: the variations and slight curvatures in the serifs, the large, round capital letters such as the "O," "U," "C," "G," and "Q," the diamond-shaped dots used for punctuation marks and over the lowercase "i" and "j," and the delicate curve to many letters such as the bottom arm of the capital "E" and "L" and lower diagonal of the lowercase "k."

Goudy Old Style is the perfect typeface to achieve a feeling of grace, elegance, or richness. It could easily be that one "especially pretty" typeface in your library. Goudy Old Style's light weight and fine hairlines make it ideal for extended text composition in catalogues, pamphlets, and brochures. These same traits make it inadvisable to reverse Goudy Old Style out of a block of solid color or use it to over-print photographs and illustrations. These design tricks require a typeface of medium or, preferably, bold weight.

dp — Goudy Old Style — Short Ascenders and Descenders

dp — Garamond — Long Ascenders and Descenders

HhMm — Slight Curve in Serifs

OUCGQ — Round Capitals

i ; • , : j — Diamond-Shaped Dots

E k L — Gentle Curve to Lower Strokes

now

Monotone in Weight

---

a

Two-Storied
Curved Stem at Baseline
Gentle Curve Where Bowl Meets Stem

R   1

Curved Tail   Bracketed Top Serif

Kk

Leg intersects diagonal at midpoint.

Condensed
Medium
Bold

Helvetica

Helvetica is available from virtually all manufacturers and by various other names, such as Helios, Megaron, and Claro. Helvetica (as it is most commonly called) is the most popular sans serif style in use today. Because of its popularity, most manufacturers are obligated to supply high-caliber versions of this face to their users. As a result, this family comes the closest to being a consistent design from all manufacturers who offer it.

Helvetica, originally named New Haas Grotesque, was first created for the Haas Type Foundry by Max Meidinger in 1957. Later, this style was adapted by the Stempel-Linotype Company for use on their equipment. At this time it was renamed "Helvetica" after the country, Helvetia (Switzerland), where the design originated.

Over the years several weights and versions have been added to the original series, and the entire family has grown to such popularity that it is a "must have" for all phototype manufacturers and users.

Helvetica is monotone in weight with only slight thinning at the intersection of character strokes. The two-stored lowercase "a" is an easy identifier for this face. The stem curves to the right at the baseline, and the bowl has a gentle curve where it intersects at the stem.

Other distinguishing characteristics of Helvetica include the curved tail of the capital "R," the bottom diagonal of the cap and lowercase "k," which connects halfway up the top diagonal, and the bracketed top serif on the numeral "1."

The Helvetica typestyle is probably read by more people in a wide variety of printed media than any other single type design, and it is used for every typesetting application imaginable. Since Helvetica is a sans serif design with strong vertical stress, try to establish close, even word spacing for maximum readability, especially when setting justified copy in a short line length. Aside from this, you should have no trouble with Helvetica. Use the condensed designs for parts lists and directories, the bold weights for strong and forceful headlines, and the medium weight for practically any application you want.

Jenson

Jenson is considered by many to be the first important roman book face, even though it has never enjoyed sustained popularity. Jenson has too much personality, too many design traits that, while making the face interesting, inhibit the reading process. The greatest contribution of Jenson to typography is as a model for other text typefaces, especially the evocative designs of William Morris and Frederic Goudy. In the early part of this century, Jenson designs were also the basis for a large family of advertising display typefaces.

Both the evocative text faces and the advertising display faces, based on the original Jenson, are currently experiencing a revival. Although the full Jenson family (first available in the 1920s) is not currently offered by phototype manufacturers, several styles are, and more are certain to come. Other popular typestyles based on Jenson design traits are Kennerley, Cloister Old Style, Centaur, and, most recently, Italia, which is available through ITC subscribers and in drytransfer lettering from Letraset International Limited.

Jenson has minor weight variations; it has strong, squared-off serifs and a "chiseled" letterform definition. The character stress is diagonal, and the top serifs of the lowercase ascenders are oblique.

A classic design trait of Jenson and typestyles patterned after it is the angled cross bar and small bowl of the lowercase "e." Other characteristics are the slanted diamond-shaped dots over the "i" and "j," the small bowl of the "a," the sharply angled link between the bowl and loop of the "g," and the geometric ear of the "r."

The capital "T" has angled serifs on the cross bar, the tail of the "R" has a slight curve, and the serifs of the "C," "E," "F," and "G" are heavily bracketed.

Jenson and its design variants run the evocative range, from vigorous and offbeat Jenson Bold Condensed to warm and friendly Italia. They are all naturals for display headlines and short to medium blocks of text composition.

Kennerley
Cloister Old Style
Centaur
Italia

Markets

Monotone Weight, Strong Serifs
Chiseled Quality to Letters
Diagonal Stress, Oblique Head-Serifs

í

Diamond-Shaped Dot

a

Small Bowl

T

Angled Serifs

R

Slight Curve to Tail

g

Sharply Angled Link

r

Geometric Ear

CEFG

Thick-Bracketed Serifs

abcdefghijklmnopqrstuvwxyz

Futura—Geometric Proportions

abcdefghijklmnopqrstuvwxyz

Kabel—Humanistic Lettering

Adrift

Terminals Cut on
Angle

a

Two-Storied
with Abbreviated Top Terminal

M

Splayed

e

Oblique Cross Bar

W

Diagonals Overlap

k

Diagonals Meet at Stem

A   B   C

Wide   Equal Bowls   Clipped Terminals

ij

Diamond-Shaped Dots

Yy

Same Design

Kabel

Most typefaces are named for type designers or are labeled with a descriptive term. Not so with Kabel. It was named in honor of an event—the laying of the first transatlantic cable. Released in 1927 (the same year as Futura), Kabel is the creation of Rudolf Koch of Germany.

While Futura is based on strict geometric proportions, Kabel's design traits can be traced to several humanistic lettering styles. Ancient Greek lapidary letters, calligraphy, and Venetian oldstyle type designs all contributed to Kabel's letterforms.

In both the capitals and lowercase, the terminals are cut on an angle. The open loop of the "g" is one of the most distinctive letters in the typeface. The lowercase "a" is two-storied and has an abbreviated top terminal. The cross bar of the "e" is very oblique, the diagonals of the "k" meet at the stem, and the "i" and "j" have diamond-shaped dots.

The capital "M" is splayed, the diagonals of the "W" overlap, and both bowls of the "B" are almost the same size, which makes the top bowl appear larger. The "A" is wide. The terminals of the "C" are clipped short, and the "Y" is a repeat of the lowercase design.

There are a number of versions of Kabel currently available; the most popular is ITC Kabel.

Kabel can be used for both text and display applications; however, its monotone weight and distinctive character designs will slightly inhibit reading in lengthy text composition. The bold and ultrabold weights of ITC Kabel are especially well suited to display typography.

Kennerley

The design of Kennerley began as a simple request for a book layout. In 1911, a British publisher, Mitchell Kennerley, approached Frederic Goudy with the proposition of creating a layout for an upcoming limited edition. Goudy took the offer and decided on a popular text design. But preliminary proofs were unsatisfactory to Goudy. As a solution he offered to design a new typeface expressly for the book at a cost far below his normal fee. Kennerley agreed; Goudy finished the new design, which he named for the publisher, late in 1911.

Taken individually, certain characters in Kennerley appear to be awkward or poorly drawn, but viewed overall the alphabet has unity and grace. Serifs are broad, concave, and slightly heavy. Weight changes are gradual, giving a monotone feel to the face.

The lowercase "a" has a flat bowl, the "e" has a diagonal cross bar, and head-serifs of the ascenders are wedge-shaped. The final stroke of the "h," "m," and "n" is slightly curved, interior diagonals of the "w" meet near the center with a heavy serif, and the "z" has vertical serifs projecting above and below the lowercase x-height.

The capital "A" and "H" have a high cross bar, the tail of the "R" has a slight curve, the "V" is wide, and the center strokes of the "W" do not cross. The diagonal of the "N" extends to the left at the top and the top serifs of the "M" extend only outward. Kennerley is another typestyle with a very fancy ampersand.

Kennerley can be used for both text and display typography. It is especially effective in blocks of large (12 point or larger) text composition.

lignite

Broad Concave Serifs
Gradual Weight Changes

a   e   hmn

Flat Bowl   Diagonal Cross Bar   Right Side Slightly Curved

bdhkl   w   z

Wedge-Shaped Head-Serifs   Middle diagonals meet at serif.   Vertical Serifs

AH   R

High Cross Bar   Slight Curve to Tail

V   W

Wide   Center strokes do not cross.

M   N

Top serifs extend outward.   Diagonal extends to left.

Fancy Ampersand

ABCDEFGHIJKLMNOPQRSTUVWXYZ
abcdefghijklmnopqrstuvwxyz

Monotone Weight, Short Serifs
Art Nouveau Influence

CG

Unusual Curve to Bowl
Tall Vertical Stroke on "G"

M

Splayed Outer Strokes
Middle Strokes Short

N

Abbreviated Diagonal

U

Unusual First Stroke

bcdgpq

Lowercase letters have the same curve as capitals. Note the lower loop of the "g."

vw

Flared, Swash-Like Strokes

ITC Korinna

The original Korinna designs were created in 1904 for the Berthold Type Foundry of Germany. Later variations of the German designs were released in America by the Intertype Company. None of these early designs, however, were especially popular. It took International Typeface Corporation (ITC) to revive this design, enlarge it into a family suitable for phototypesetting, and popularize Korinna as we now know it. Ed Benguiat of ITC is responsible for adding the first true italic designs of ITC Korinna Kursiv to the family. Actually, so many refinements and weight additions have been added to the original Berthold creation that the current designs should be considered more of a re-creation than a revival.

ITC Korinna is monotone in weight, has short serifs, and a definite Art Nouveau quality to the design. This typestyle abounds with distinguishing characteristics. The capital "C" and "G" have an unusually curved bowl, and the "G" has a tall vertical stroke. The cap "M" is splayed, and the middle strokes descend only partway to the baseline. The capital "N" has an abbreviated diagonal, and the capital "U" an unusual bow to the first stroke. The lowercase x-height is quite large. The lowercase "b," "c," "d," "g," "p," and "q" all share the same unusual curved bowl found in the capitals. The "g" has a distinctive curve to the lower loop, while the "v" and "w" of ITC Korinna Kursiv have a flared, almost swash, quality.

One of the hallmarks of a truly versatile typestyle is that it can be used equally well for text and display applications. ITC Korinna has this ability.

Melior

Melior is one of the three most important type designs created by Swiss designer Hermann Zapf (the other two are Optima and Palatino). It was originally intended to be a newspaper typestyle in 1948 and has since become a mainstay of current typography. In many ways, Melior is an unusual type design. Although engineered to be highly legible, it also has very distinctive qualities not normally found in a single design. Melior is one of the few popular Egyptian, or square serif, typestyles to have a strong weight stress.

Melior is a relatively square design, with a large and somewhat condensed lowercase. These qualities contribute good visibility and space conservation. Although strictly classified as a square serif typestyle, the serifs in Melior are slightly rounded. The capital "A" has a high cross bar and a flat top, and the center strokes of the capital "W" meet at the top of the character. The lowercase "f" has a tight pot-hook, and the link between the bowl and loop of the lowercase "g" is almost a straight line. The lowercase "y" looks like a "v" with the second diagonal extended and curved. The top of the lowercase "t" is sheared. The italic is basically the roman typestyle obliqued, except for the "a," "f," and "k."

Melior mixes well with square serif designs like Egyptian or Stymie, and sans serif typestyles such as Univers and Antique Olive. Discretion should be exercised when attempting to mix Melior with some stressed serif typestyles; many times there are not enough design differences to achieve contrast. For example, ITC Korinna or Trump Mediaeval will not mix as well with Melior as will Times Roman or several of the Goudy variants.

Direct mail pieces, booklets, magazines, and brochures—any medium that calls for a combination of distinction and readability—can be set in Melior.

Mom

Large, Slightly Condensed Lowercase
Note serifs.

afk

Design in Melior italic
differs from roman.

AW

Apex of "A" and "W"
Flat

fg

Tight Pot-Hook on "f"
Unusual Link of Bowl and Loop of "g"

vy

The first stroke of the "y" does
not close with the stem.

Egyptian Bold Condensed
Stymie Bold
Antique Olive
Univers
Goudy Old Style
Times Roman

Good Mixers with Melior

Trump Mediaeval
ITC Korinna

Not-So-Good Mixers
with Melior

acgm

Baskerville

acgm

Optima

Classic Character Designs and
Proportions Without Serifs

giraffe

Stressed Weights
Slight Flare Where Serif Would Be

M S EFL

Splayed	Slight Forward Tilt	Narrow

g a

Very Wide Open Counters
Ear of "g" Parallel with Baseline
Terminal of "a" Not Flared

R   J

Tail joins almost at stem.	Descends below baseline.

fr

Narrow

N N

Diagonal Heavy

hijk

Dots Below Ascenders

Optima

Hermann Zapf designed Optima because he felt a redrawn sixteenth-century book face or an updated nineteenth-century sans serif were insufficient to reflect the progress attained in the twentieth century. He wanted to create a typestyle that would satisfy the needs of modern communication. Optima is a serif-less roman typestyle: classic letterforms without serifs. While this kind of design was not totally new to typography, prior to Optima it had not been taken to successful completion. Although the design was begun in 1952, the finished typeface was not available until 1958. Truly a product of the twentieth century, the italic for Optima was one of the first text typestyles to be developed through a photographic distortion system.

Optima is easily identified; it is one of the most beautiful sans serif designs you'll run across. Character strokes have stressed weights and flair slightly where a serif would normally be.

The capital "M" is splayed, the "S" has a slight forward tilt, and the "E," "F," and "L" are narrow. The tail of the "R" joins almost at the stem, the "J" descends below the baseline, and the diagonal of the "N" is heavy as in a classic serif design.

Lowercase counters are large and open. The ear of the "g" is parallel with the baseline. The "f" and "r" are narrow. The terminal of the "a" is not flared as are others in the face. The dots over the "i" and "j" are somewhat smaller and sit lower than the ascenders.

Optima is a must for all commercial type libraries. Its applications are too numerous to mention and it mixes well with almost all serif and sans serif typestyles. Optima is one of my, and Hermann Zapf's, favorite designs.

Palatino

Palatino was the first major type design to be created by Hermann Zapf. It is also his most popular design. Drawn in the late 1940s, it was initially released to the public in 1950 by the Stempel Type Foundry of Germany. Palatino's calligraphic style is based on the work of Italian Renaissance type designers, and is a careful mixture of contemporary and oldstyle design qualities. Open, wide letterforms characterize this typestyle and, although unusual curves are present in several characters, the overall feel of the face is one of grace and elegance.

The capital "A" has a high cross bar and is very wide at the base. The bowl of the capital "D" pulls to the upper right, as do those of the "P" and "R." The "P" and "R" also have an open bowl at their bases. The capital "Y" is splayed, has no top serifs, and tapers on the second diagonal. The cap "K" has a long lower diagonal, and Palatino's hallmark, the capital "S," has an unusually curved spine.

The lowercase "e" has a large top counter and a small angle at the end of the bowl which imitates a broad pen stroke. The lowercase "h," "m," and "n" have only half-serifs on the final stroke. The stem of the lowercase "t" is quite tall and the "g" is wide with closely spaced bowl and loop.

Hermann Zapf originally intended Palatino to be used for commercial printing, but its popularity and success with advertisers and book designers has extended its versatility. Palatino is equally effective in both text and display applications; however, it works best in larger sizes in setting text composition. When used in too small a size, some manufacturers' versions of Palatino tend to look somewhat heavy. Palatino will add a classic, elegant feeling to typography and is useful for almost all typesetting applications.

DPR

Distinctive Curve to Bowl
''P'' and ''R'' Bowl Not Closed

S A K

Palatino's Hallmark

High Cross Bar
Wide at Base

Long Diagonal

Y

Splayed
No Top Serifs
Second Diagonal Tapers

hmn

Half-Serifs on Final Stroke

e t

Large Top Counter

Tall Stem

g

Wide with
Closely Spaced Bowl
and Loop

Cheltenham Bold
Franklin Gothic
News Gothic
Stymie Medium

Designs of Morris Benton

ITC Souvenir Light
ITC Souvenir Light Italic
ITC Souvenir Medium
ITC Souvenir Medium Italic
ITC Souvenir Demi
ITC Souvenir Demi Italic
ITC Souvenir Bold
ITC Souvenir Bold Italic

e

Diagonal Stress

p

Bottom of Bowl Open

g

Open Loop

v y w

Curved Strokes

B R

Angled Cross Bars
and Curved Tail

ITC Souvenir

Souvenir was originally drawn in the year 1914 by one of America's most prolific type designers, Morris Benton. Over two hundred typeface designs are credited to this man; faces such as Alternate Gothic, most of the Cheltenham family, News Gothic, Century Expanded, Franklin Gothic, Stymie family, and Wedding Text are just a few.

Unfortunately, Souvenir was not a popular design when it was originally released by the American Type Founders Company (ATF). However, the people at International Typeface Corporation (ITC) saw the potential popularity of this warm, friendly type and were granted a license to the name and basic design from ATF in 1970.

Ed Benguiat of ITC took the single weight designed by Mr. Benton and expanded it into a complete type family suitable for phototypography.

The ITC Souvenir family is easily identified since there is no other typeface currently being used that looks quite like it. The lowercase is round and large with several distinctive characters. The bowl of the "e" is diagonal and rounded, the loop of the "g" is open, the "v," "w," and "y" have soft curves rather than straight diagonal strokes, and the bottom of the bowl on the "p" does not quite close. The capital "W," "V," and "Y" share the same soft curves as their lowercase counterparts. The cross bars on the "B" and "R" are angled rather than horizontal, the "R" also having a curved tail.

ITC Souvenir is suitable for both text and display applications. Both the light and medium weights work well in extended text settings; however, the medium requires a little extra line space to avoid a heavy-appearing page. All weights are well suited to display work and will give a casual, friendly air to headlines. The bold weight will add extra emphasis where you need it most, while the lighter weights create a feeling of sensitivity.

Stymie

Stymie, Memphis, Cairo, Karnak, and Egyptienne—names that conjure up pictures of the Nile and ancient Egypt—are typestyles categorized as Egyptian. They share common design traits of monotone stroke weight and strong squared-off serifs. This generic type was first designed in the early nineteenth century for advertising purposes. An important news event at this time was the discovery of the Rosetta Stone of the ancient Egyptians. When the Rosetta Stone was first brought to London, it made it possible to decipher Egyptian hieroglyphics. Egyptology became an enthusiastic and popular interest that coincided with the introduction of the square-serif typestyles. The term used to describe these designs was coined then and is still in use today.

Since its origin in England, the Egyptian style has been reproduced in many different versions. Stymie was first designed by Morris Benton in 1931 for the American Type Founders Company as a text and display variation on the standard Egyptian theme.

The serifs are the same weight as the stems and are unbracketed. The capital "A" normally has a slab serif at the apex. The capital "G" has a spur, and the middle strokes of the capital "M" stop short of the baseline. The lowercase "a" is supplied in either a one- or two-storied design, depending on the type founder. The lowercase "g" follows sans serif designs and the lowercase "t" has a foot-serif to the right only.

Egyptian display typestyles have been popular since their introduction, adding a sense of authority and weight to headlines. However, the incidence of setting text composition in this style has varied over the years. Currently, it is quite common to see annual reports, advertising circulars, and other ephemeral printing set in Stymie. The lighter weights work best in small sizes, are easy to read, and add personality to short blocks of text composition. Stymie is also one of the few typestyles that can be reversed out of a dark background in text sizes and still maintain high levels of readability.

A

Slab Serif at Apex

G

Spur Serif

M

Middle Strokes Just Short of Baseline

a

Two-Storied "a"
(Stymie Medium)

α

One-Storied "a"
(Stymie Bold)

g

Sans Serif
Design

t

Foot-Serif
to Right

abcdefghijklmnopqrstuvwxyz

Tall and Slightly Condensed Lowercase

c e

Weight Stress Angled and Low

ikm

Head-Serifs Angled

C P B

Barbed Peak   Bowl   Lower bowl
               turns up   appears too small.
               slightly.

Times Roman

Originally designed for newspapers, Times Roman has become the most popular, serviceable typestyle in both the United States and England. Unlike other typefaces, it was designed by committee. Stanley Morison provided the original drawings to the London *Times* newspaper when they decided to restyle their format in 1931. However, his penciled renderings went through many design changes before the staff of *The Times,* and the experts they hired, were satisfied.

Times Roman is as appropriate for setting very fine typography as it is for the more humble jobs. The large lowercase x-height and somewhat condensed design save space and maintain high levels of readability and legibility. Because it is slightly heavier than most serif text designs, Times Roman can survive poor printing conditions.

The weight stress of the lowercase is at an angle, and is especially low on the lowercase "c" and "e." The head-serifs (or top serifs) of letters "i," "k," and "m" are angled as in Baskerville. The upper terminal of the cap "C" has a barbed peak and the lower ends in a point. The bowl of the cap "P" turns up slightly as it meets the stem, and the lower bowl of the cap "B" appears too small. All of the capital letters share small fine-pointed serifs.

Times Roman is considered a universal type. It is a "must" for every typesetter's library.

Univers

Developed in 1956, Univers is a milestone in modern type invention. It's one of the first typeface families that was completely planned and designed before any faces went into production. The ability to preplan type design has only been possible with the technology of phototypesetting. Because of the manufacturing expense of hot metal type reproduction, type foundries did not always extend a type family beyond the basic series. Variations were added later, based on the popularity of the initial release. Many times, this "growing like Topsy" effect caused design inconsistencies within a type family.

Although it is easily confused with Helvetica, Univers may be distinguished by many characters. Most obvious is the lowercase "a," which has almost no curve to its vertical stroke, and a horizontal connection where the top of the bowl meets the stem.

The intersection of the diagonals on the lowercase and capital "K" is at the point where they join the vertical stroke.

The capital "G" has a long vertical stem and does not have the spur found on the same character in Helvetica.

Univers is also not so monotone a design as Helvetica. The more pronounced stress to the stroke weights in Univers makes it more readable in long blocks of text copy.

A large family consisting of twenty-one variants, Univers offers a wide range of faces for both text and display applications. There is a version for practically every typesetting need; this can be especially valuable when trying to add continuity to a complicated job with many typographic requirements.

a

Helvetica

a

Univers
Very Little Curve to Vertical Stroke
No Curve and a Horizontal Connection
Where Top of Bowl Meets Stem

G

Helvetica

G

Univers
Long Vertical Stem
No Spur

Kk

Diagonals meet at the vertical stroke.

now

Helvetica

now

Univers
Pronounced Stress
to Strokes

Univers Family

Novelty faces

Some novelty faces have become classics in their own right, while others are fad-faces that have a short life span. The typefaces covered here are proven winners, faces you can use for many years.

iw

Typewriter Type Monospaced

iw

Typefaces Proportional

ITC American Typewriter

There have been typestyles that emulate typewriter type since the typewriter was invented. Technologically, this is roughly akin to airing radio programs (with no pictures) on television.

Typewriter type is monospaced (each character, whether it's a lowercase "i" or a capital "W," takes up the same amount of space). While this kind of standardization may be good for machine design, it is poor typographic design.

The first typewriter was manufactured in 1874, and shortly thereafter the first typewriter-like typeface was released by an American type foundry. It was created to give printed pieces the immediacy and personalism found in typewritten copy.

ITC American Typewriter does all this —and more. Although it has the look and feel of typewritten copy, the character design and spacing are proportional, increasing both legibility and readability.

ITC American Typewriter is also softer and friendlier than a strict copy of typewriter type. The medium version of this six-weight family works surprisingly well for extended text composition. The bold shares similar design traits with Cheltenham Bold, while the light could almost pass as a Stymie.

How do you identify ITC American Typewriter? Well, it looks as if it was set with a typewriter—only better.

ABCDEFGHIJKLMNOPQRSTUVWXYZ
abcdefghijklmnopqrstuvwxyz

Typewriter Type

ABCDEFGHIJKLMNOPQRSTUVWXYZ
abcdefghijklmnopqrstuvwxyz

ITC American Typewriter

park

Cheltenham Bold

graphic

Stymie Light

park

ITC American Typewriter Bold

graphic

ITC American Typewriter Light

image

ITC Bauhaus

image

Gill Sans—Sans Serif with Classic Configurations

abdgpq

Bowls Which Do Not Quite Close

mnu

Single-Stroke Design

W CASLON JUNR

Caslon Sans Serif

abcdefghi klmnopqrs

Bayer's Universal Alphabet

ITC Bauhaus

The first sans serif typeface was released in 1816 by the Caslon Type Foundry of England. It contained only capital letters and was not particularly popular. This first design was intended primarily for display purposes. In the early 1900s, type founders began to introduce sans serif designs for text usage that were of a higher design quality than their predecessors. It is these faces that serve as the standard for current sans serif typestyles.

In England, sans serif designs essentially were patterned after serif typestyles. The weight stresses and character designs were classic roman serif configurations with the absence of serifs. Gill Sans is a perfect example. The Germans, however, took a different approach. Their alphabets showed more structural and geometric forms, with the intent of achieving a modular unity based on strict geometric shapes. One of the most representative examples of this school of thought is the "Universal Alphabet" designed by Herbert Bayer at the Bauhaus in 1925.

ITC Bauhaus was inspired by Herbert Bayer's design. Mr. Bayer felt that a true universal typestyle should be common case (no distinction between capitals and lowercase). Since this convention never caught on, ITC included capital character designs to complement the lowercase.

ITC Bauhaus can be easily spotted by its extreme monotone weight and strict adherence to geometric forms. In the lowercase, the bowls of the "a," "b," "d," "g," "p," and "q" do not quite close. The lowercase "n" and "u" are single-stroke characters with no main stem. The "m" follows the same style. The lowercase and capital "S" are flat on top and bottom, while the capital and lowercase "X" are created from curved strokes. The capital "E" has a curved vertical stroke. The "L" has a radiused connection between horizontal and vertical strokes. The horizontal strokes of the "A," "B," "P," and "R" do not reach the stem.

Although based on a design dating to the 1920s, ITC Bauhaus has the contemporary look of computers and integrated circuits.

ITC has designed the Bauhaus family for both text and display applications. However, the monotone weight and unusual character designs do not make ITC Bauhaus ideally suited to extended text composition. Although there are several other typestyles available that emulate the universal alphabet of Bayer, none are as successful or well integrated as ITC Bauhaus.

Ss

Flat on Top and Bottom

Xx

Curved Strokes

EL

Curved Strokes

ABPR

Horizontals Which Do Not Quite Meet Stem

Caslon Antique

The interesting thing about Caslon Antique is that it is neither a Caslon nor a true antique design. This typeface was first released by the Barnhart Brothers and Spindler Type Foundry in the late 1800s and called "Fourteenth Century."

The rugged design was created to give the appearance of the first roman typefaces cast after Gutenberg. When the management at Barnhart Brothers and Spindler became embarrassingly aware that Gutenberg did not do his work until the middle of the fifteenth century, they changed the name of their new, old design to "Fifteenth Century."

Fifteenth Century was moderately popular until the early 1920s when its name was again changed—to Caslon Antique. At that time, the phrase "when in doubt, set it in Caslon" was the byword of typesetters, attesting to its popularity. It was hoped that the name change would increase the sales and usage of this design. It did—and Caslon Antique has been a popular novelty face ever since.

The first clue to identifying Caslon Antique is the rugged, rough-hewn edges of the characters. A second clue is the obviously uneven character heights.

Specific characters to look for are the condensed lowercase "a," "n," and "u." The lowercase "e" has a very high cross bar; the "j" appears shorter than the other lowercase characters. The capital "R" is condensed, the capital "Q" has a short tail, and the top horizontal on the capital "E" is longer than the others. The "A" has a very high cross bar.

Although a display design, limited usage of Caslon Antique in text sizes creates a feeling of antiquity. This typestyle is also very easy to overuse; a little Caslon Antique goes a long way.

Antiques

Rough Edges and Uneven Character Heights

e   ijn

High Cross Bar   "j" Short

R   Q   E   A

Condensed   Short Tail   Top Horizontal Long   High Cross Bar

Packard

Cooper's First Design

bock

Oldstyle Design Characteristics
of Cooper Black

Goudy Heavy
Cooper Black

eg **eg** **n**

Rounded Serifs

A **A** **ij**

Elliptical Dots

T **T** **f**

ITC Souvenir Bold   Cooper Black   Distinctive Pot-Hook

Cooper Black

Chicago and the 1920s were responsible for a lot more than the proliferation of bathtub gin and Al Capone. The great American boldface—Cooper Black—was also a product of this time and place. It was created by Oswald Cooper, one of America's most gifted type designers.

Several typestyles and many examples of hand lettering are the product of Oz Cooper's handiwork. In fact, his first typeface, Packard, was the outgrowth of advertising lettering he did for the Packard Motor Car Company. The face for which he is most remembered, however, is Cooper Black.

When it was first cast in metal, Cooper Black gave true meaning to the term "weight" for describing a typeface design. In a 120-point font, the capital "W" alone weighed almost a pound!

Although barely recognizable, Cooper Black is actually based on oldstyle characteristics. The axis of the curves is inclined to the left, serifs are bracketed, and the serifs of the lowercase ascenders are oblique. Cooper Black can easily be confused with two other popular typestyles, Goudy Heavy and ITC Souvenir Bold. Goudy Heavy, however, is more structured and has much smaller serifs than Cooper Black. ITC Souvenir Bold is a closer design match, but several characters distinguish the two faces. In the lowercase, the "e" and "g" in Cooper Black are the standard roman designs. In the capitals, the apex of the "A" bends to the left and overlaps the first diagonal, and the "T" has much more pronounced serifs in Cooper than in ITC Souvenir.

Other distinguishing characteristics of Cooper Black are the serifs that are rounded, rather than flat on top and bottom, the elliptical dots over the lowercase "i" and "j," and the distinctive pot-hook of the lowercase "f."

Cooper Black is a friendly display face that not only adds weight and impact to headlines, but also a feeling of warmth. Because of its extreme weight and small counters, Cooper Black is obviously not suited to text composition.

ITC Gorilla

ITC Gorilla was part of the first group of display typefaces released by International Typeface Corporation. If Palatino or Goudy Old Style elicit feelings of beauty and elegance, ITC Gorilla will make the reader think of things rugged or maybe ugly. This "ugly" typestyle can, however, be traced back to prestigious beginnings.

ITC Gorilla is a phototype adaptation of a typeface called Roycroft, originally designed in the late 1890s. It was one of the first type designs of Morris Fuller Benton, the man responsible for approximately two hundred typestyles. Roycroft is also reputed to be the first typeface that was cut directly by the pantograph machine, a piece of equipment that revolutionized the type industry at the turn of the nineteenth century.

The most obvious clue to identifying ITC Gorilla is its rough character edges. The face is almost monotone in weight with short, stubby serifs. Lowercase characters are generally condensed. The lowercase "b," "d," "p," and "q" have an unusual bowl design, similar to ITC Korinna. The capital and lowercase "v" are quite wide. The capital "E" has a long lower arm, the "D," "M," and "R" are condensed, and the "U" has an awkward curve that is repeated nowhere else in the alphabet. For a rugged, ugly typestyle, ITC Gorilla has a very fancy ampersand.

While the uses for ITC Gorilla may not be as varied as other typestyles, it is nevertheless a good "bin filler" for a display library. It will lend a feeling of strength and power to advertising headlines and energy to display composition.

Fancy Ampersand

mashed

Rough Edges, Monotone Weight, Stubby Serifs

bdpq

Unusual Bowls

DMR

Condensed

Roycroft from A.T.F.

E

Long Lower Arm

Vv

Wide

U

Awkward Curve

style

Bold with Short Ascenders and Descenders

RM

Condensed

CT

Similar Design

---

h cfrs ij

Flag-Like Terminals and Dots

---

a **uv** **Zz**

Two-Storied   Easily Confused   Cross Bar

Old English

Old English is an example of the most ancient style of type used in the Western world. It is patterned after the lettering produced in northern Europe just prior to Gutenberg. This style of type is known by many other names; it is called "black letter" by some because of its heavy, dominant, vertical strokes. Typefaces of this kind are also referred to as "text," from the Latin *textura*, alluding to the close-woven texture of a page set in this style; and "gothic," after the tall-spired churches of medieval Europe. The name "Old English" is derived from the fifteenth-century typefaces that William Caxton developed in England.

Old English is a very bold face, with short ascenders and descenders. It is not especially readable or legible, and normally should be avoided for extended text composition. There are no absolute rules in typography, but if there were, "Never set all-capital headlines in Old English" would head the list.

Although typefaces of the Old English style are easy to spot, specific designs are sometimes hard to differentiate. In all typefaces of this kind, the lowercase characters are condensed, with each letter taking up approximately the same space. The strong vertical strokes are connected by hairlines, usually drawn at an angle. The capitals are customarily expanded and very ornate. The complicated and decorative design of the capitals is an attempt at better legibility—to distinguish caps from lowercase characters.

Specifically, Old English can be distinguished from other similar typestyles by looking closely at one or more characters. The lowercase "h" has a small flag at the base of the right stroke. Terminals of the "c," "f," "r," and "s" are also flaglike designs, as are the dots over the "i" and "j." Although the lowercase "a" is two-storied, because of its configuration it appears to be a one-storied design. The lowercase "u" and "v" can be easily confused, and the "z," in both capital and lowercase form, has a cross bar. Capitals are almost square and have the same flag motif found in the lowercase. The capital "R" and "M" are condensed compared to the other capitals. The "C" and "T" are similar in design.

While Old English is overused in antique store advertising and theological announcements, it is a striking typestyle that can be an effective display type if used with discretion. It also mixes well with most text serif typestyles.

Raphael

Raphael is one of the many thousands of novelty typefaces created in the latter part of the nineteenth century. It was one of several designed by William F. Jackson for the Central Type Foundry of St. Louis. After doing service for the better half of a century, one of the original fonts found its way into the antique type collection of T. J. Lyons in Boston, Massachusetts.

Compugraphic Corporation saw potential in the design when they purchased the T. J. Lyons collection in 1974. Raphael was updated to current typographic standards and released later the same year. The most obvious design change was the removal of the interior shading of character strokes, which dated the original typestyle.

Raphael is now available in dry-transfer sheets from Letraset International Limited of England.

The design is slightly bold in weight, with condensed capitals and a comparatively large lowercase x-height. Serifs are thin and seem to truncate the flared vertical strokes. The round lowercase characters have a diagonal weight stress similar to oldstyle designs.

The "m" and "n" have an almost swash design and the counter of the "e" is quite large. The "o" appears to be made with the stroke of a brush and is open at the top. The capital "O," "Q," and numeral zero are also open at the top. Many of the capitals have a swash quality. The "M" is condensed. The capital "U" and "J" have small spurs where the verticals curve at the base of the character (this is a holdover from Raphael's antique origin).

Raphael has a warm, cheerful look to it, and is ideal for headlines and short blocks of display composition. The fancy design of the capitals, however, prohibits all-capital composition.

Original Raphael

Current Design

Europe

Thin Serifs, Flared Verticals, Diagonal Stress

mn

Swash Strokes

o

Brush Stroke

e

Large Counter

OQO

Open at Top

ANP

Fancy Capitals

M

Condensed

JU

Small Spurs

SANS SERIF SHADED
UNCLE BILL

Spur and Tapered Terminal   Tapered Terminals   Sheared

BINNER

Middle Arm High   Unusual Cross Bar   Diagonals meet high on stroke.

Large Bowls   Tall Vertical and No Spur   Diagonals appear misdesigned.

SANS SERIF SHADED

Sans Serif Shaded is really more important as a novelty typestyle than a particular typeface, since there are many faces that share similar design traits. The two most popular are the original Sans Serif Shaded and a typeface called Uncle Bill or Uncle Sam Open.

Sans Serif Shaded was designed in 1839 by William Thorowgood; Uncle Bill was created over a hundred years later in the 1960s. The three-dimensional quality of these two typestyles seems to attract reader attention in display typography.

Sans Serif Shaded is a capitals-only typestyle, and the letters are all approximately the same width. The "G" has a spur (common to nineteenth-century sans serif designs), and round characters appear somewhat short because they are not much taller than flat characters. The "C," "G," and "J" taper at the terminals, and the numeral one has a sheared top.

Uncle Bill was adapted from another nineteenth-century design, a typeface called Binner. A California-based company, now called FotoStar International, utilized phototechnology to produce an outline and drop shadow version from the original Binner. Although also a sans serif design, Uncle Bill has much more weight stress than Sans Serif Shaded. The middle arm of the "E" and "F" is quite high, as is the unusual cross bar of the "H." The two diagonals of the "K" meet high on the stem. The "P" and "R" have unusually large bowls. The "G" has no spur, but has a tall vertical stroke. The "M" appears to be poorly designed.

There are other Sans Serif Shaded designs to choose from. Most would make valuable additions to a display library. These two just happen to be my favorites.

ITC Serif Gothic

ITC Serif Gothic was first released in 1972 by International Typeface Corporation. The original designs for this typeface were a joint effort by Herb Lubalin and Antonio Dispigna. Only two designs (regular and bold) were part of the initial release; the remaining five weights and the outline now available were released in 1974.

As the name implies, ITC Serif Gothic is essentially a stylized gothic (sans serif) design with the addition of small serifs. In fact, in small text sizes the serifs almost disappear. The reason that this typestyle and Old English are both referred to as gothic is that when sans serif typestyles were first introduced in America they were called "gothics"; no one is quite sure why. Perhaps it is because these first bold display faces resembled faces like Old English. The term stuck, and in America faces without serifs can either be referred to as "sans serif" or "gothic."

As with all ITC designs, the lowercase x-height is quite large. ITC Serif Gothic shares many design similarities with ITC Bauhaus. There are also several alternate and swash characters, which have been made available through most phototype equipment manufacturers.

Individual lowercase letters with distinguishing characteristics are the "c" and "e," which have clipped terminals, the "t," which has a short, sheared stem, and the "v" and "w," which are wide.

In the capitals, the bowls of the "B" do not meet at the stem, the "M" is splayed, and the "W" is an unusual design in that the second diagonal is truncated. Compared with lowercase proportions, the capital "S" and "Z" are condensed. The "G" shares the same clipped terminals as the lowercase "c" and "e." The numeral one has a long diagonal stroke, and the zero is condensed compared with other round characters.

While ITC Serif Gothic is a little too distinctive to qualify as a general purpose text typestyle, short blocks of text composition can be effective in the right application. Because of its exceptionally small serifs, ITC Serif Gothic can also be set tightly with little fear of characters overlapping or creating poor typographic color.

gmr

ITC Serif Gothic

gmr

ITC Bauhaus

efkmn
aefhkkmnstyz
aA@eemnQrz

Alternate and Swash Characters

ce	t	vw
Clipped Terminals	Short, Sheared Stem	Wide Proportions

M	W	B
Splayed	Truncated Second Diagonal	Bowls do not meet stem.

SZ	G	1	0
Condensed	Clipped Terminal	Long Diagonal	Condensed

ITC Souvenir

Clearface Gothic

Souvenir Gothic

Walbaum

Melior

Bodoni

ITC Zapf Book

Typestyle Blends

Caxton

Ronaldson

ITC Tiffany is a contemporary blend of these.

ITC Tiffany

The long serifs and strong weight contrast.

hmnu

Abrupt Shoulders

k

Leg overlaps diagonal.

g

Open Loop

e

Oblique Cross Bar

ABMNYZ

Wide diagonals
overlap hairlines.

G

Slight Spur

T

Top Serifs
Splayed

EFL

Spur serifs extend
beyond cap
and baseline.

ITC Tiffany

Several typestyles in popular use were created by combining the designs of two or more different typefaces. Type Spectra's Souvenir Gothic combines the design traits of ITC Souvenir and Clearface Gothic. ITC Zapf Book blends the characteristics of Walbaum, Melior, and Bodoni.

ITC Tiffany is another such typestyle. It is a contemporary blend of two typefaces—Ronaldson and Caxton—designed over seventy-five years ago. Ronaldson was released by MacKeller, Smiths and Jordan, an outgrowth of the oldest type foundry in America. Caxton was a product of the American Type Founders Company.

The most distinguishing feature of ITC Tiffany (and its two ancestral designs) is its very long and graceful serifs. Another characteristic is the strong weight contrast between thick and thin strokes. This contrast is as pronounced as Bodoni's, but much more graceful. The lowercase x-height is large and the counters are open. Similar to Baskerville, the lower loop of the "g" does not quite close. The shoulders of the "h," "m," "n," and "u" are abrupt and do not imitate the soft curves found elsewhere in the alphabet. The lower diagonal of the "k" overlaps the upper hairline diagonal, and the cross bar of the "e" is oblique.

Generally, the capitals are wide and the diagonal strokes overlap their intersection hairlines. The top serifs of the "T" are splayed and the "G" has a slight spur. The spur serifs on the arms of the "E," "F," and "L" extend above the cap height and below the baseline.

Because of its long serifs and extreme weight contrast, ITC Tiffany should be handled with care in text composition. If it is set too tightly the serifs will touch, and the weight contrast tends to make long passages difficult to read. For advertising, display typography, or short blocks of text copy, Tiffany is an excellent choice.

University Roman

University Roman is certainly not one of the world's more important type designs; however, it possesses charm and distinction.

University Roman was first called Stunt Roman and was an example of hand lettering. The alphabet dates back to 1937 and owes its origin to the humble Speedball lettering pen. In conjunction with their product line of artist's pens, the Speedball Company published an idea-book for young designers. University Roman was first shown in one of these books and titled Stunt Roman.

University Roman wasn't actually type until Lettergraphics, a phototypesetting service in California, spotted the design, saw merit in it, and released it into their library in the late 1960s. A little later, Letraset International Limited of England also saw the design and converted it for use on dry-transfer sheets. Since then, a bold weight and italic design, in addition to the original roman, have been made available to phototypesetting manufacturers.

University Roman can be identified by the unusually large bowls on the capital "P," "R," and lowercase "g." The capital "E," "F," "H," "M," "N," and "U" are very condensed and contrast to the full-bodied "C," "D," "G," "O," "Q," and "S." The lowercase "a" and "f" have an unusual overhang, the "m" is condensed, and the "t" has a large loop to the right. The serifs of all the characters are straight hairline strokes and are, in some cases, quite long. The ampersand of this typeface is especially pretty.

University Roman when used in display sizes is well suited for greeting cards, announcements, menus, and other forms of ephemeral printing.

&

Ampersand

P g R

Large Bowls

E F H M N U

Very Condensed

Stunt Roman
from Speedball
Book of 1930s

C D G O Q S

Full-Bodied

af   m   t

Unusual Overhang   Condensed   Large Loop

Appendix

Typeface analogue:
a cross-reference to other names for the specific typestyles

The following reference has been compiled to make life easier for typographers, typesetters, and graphic designers. Extensive research and trained typographic eyes have produced this guide that cross-references the different names for the most used and/or most confused typestyles. The information presented here is more complete and accurate than all known previous lists of this type.

The guide relates to the typestyle of major manufacturers of keyboard or tape-driven phototypesetters. Where the manufacturer was known for a particular typeface name, it is indicated. Typestyles known by the same name (as with ITC Benguiat) and available from virtually all manufacturers are omitted. Typestyles generally available from only one manufacturer, such as Compugraphic's **Holland Seminar**, are also omitted.

It is a fact that typeface names and designs can change from manufacturer to manufacturer. Design adaptations have always been present in the typographic industry: faces originally cut for handset type were adapted to phototype, and adaptations are made to convert a face for use on one phototypesetter to another. Through each generation the typeface can, and usually does, have design changes. This means that typefaces as they were originally conceived and drawn are not what we are using and specifying today. Major manufacturers spend much time and expense creating accurate versions of popular typestyles for their customers. In many cases, however, they give the completed design a new name.

Armed with this guide, you can successfully determine and cross-reference the various names given to a particular typestyle. The judgment of design quality ultimately rests with you.

A Guide to Abbreviations		
Autologic Incorporated	**AI**
Alphatype Corporation	**Alpha**
AM International Varityper Division	**AM**
H. Berthold AG	**BH**
Compugraphic Corporation	**CG**
Dymo Graphic Systems Incorporated	**Dymo**
Harris Composition Systems Harris Corporation	**HC**
International Business Machines	**IBM**
Itek Graphic Products	**Itek**
Mergenthaler Linotype Corporation	**Merg**
Wang Graphic Systems, Incorporated	**Wang**

A

Ad Bold (AI, Dymo)
    Casual
    Dom Casual (CG)
    Polka (BH)

AG (Itek)
    ITC Avant Garde Gothic (AI, Alpha, AM, BH, CG, Dymo, HC, Merg)
    Cadence
    Suave (Wang)

Airport
    Europe
    FU (Itek)
    Futura (Alpha, BH, CG, HC, Merg)
    Photura (AI, Dymo)
    Sirius
    Spartan (Merg)
    Techno (AI, AM, Dymo)
    Tempo
    Twentieth Century
    Utica (Wang)

Aldine Roman (IBM)
    Bem (CG)
    Bembo (AI, AM, BH, Dymo, Merg, Wang)
    Griffo (Alpha)

Alexandria (Wang)
    Cairo (HC)
    Memphis (Merg)
    Pyramid (IBM)
    ST (Itek)
    Stymie (AI, Alpha, AM, BH, CG, Dymo)

Alpha Gothic (Alpha)
    Classified News Medium (IBM)
    News Gothic (AI, Alpha, BH, CG, Dymo, HC, Wang)
    Toledo
    Trade Gothic (Merg)

Alphavers (Alpha)
    Aries
    Boston (Wang)
    Galaxy (HC)
    UN (Itek)
    Univers (AI, AM, BH, CG, Dymo, IBM, Merg)
    Versatile (Alpha)

Alpin Gothic (CG)
    Alternate Gothic (AI, AM, HC, Merg, Wang)

Alternate Gothic (AI, AM, HC, Merg, Wang)
    Alpin Gothic (CG)

Americana (BH, Merg)
    American Classic (CG)
    Colonial (AM)

American Classic (CG)
    Americana (BH, Merg)
    Colonial (AM)

American Uncial (BH)
    Uncial (CG)

Andover (AI, AM, Dymo)
    Elegante (HC)
    Malibu (AI)
    Paladium (CG)
    Palatino (BH, Merg)
    Patina (Alpha)
    Pontiac (Wang)

Antique Olive (BH, CG, Merg)
    Oliva
    Olive (AM)
    Olivette
    Olivette Antique (Wang)

Anzeigen Grotesk (BH)
    Aura (CG)
    Aurora (Alpha)
    Aurora Bold Condensed
    Grotesque Condensed (Dymo)

Aquarius
    Corona (Merg)
    CR (Itek)
    Crown (AI, AM, Dymo)
    Koronna (Alpha)
    News No. 3, 9 pt., 8 set (CG)
    News No. 5, 5.5 pt., 6 set (CG)
    News No. 6, 8 pt., 8 set (CG)
    Nimbus (AI)
    Quincy
    Royal (HC)
    Vela

Aries
    Alphavers (Alpha)
    Boston (Wang)
    Galaxy (HC)
    UN (Itek)
    Univers (AI, AM, BH, CG, Dymo, IBM, Merg)
    Versatile (Alpha)

Aster (BH, CG, Merg)
    Astro (Alpha, Wang)
    Aztec (AI)

Astro (Alpha, Wang)
    Aster (BH, CG, Merg)
    Aztec (AI)

Atlantic (Alpha)
    PL (Itek)
    Planet (Wang)
    Plantin (AI, AM, BH, CG, Dymo, Merg)

Aura (CG)
    Anzeigen Grotesk (BH)
    Aurora (Alpha)
    Aurora Bold Condensed
    Grotesque Condensed (Dymo)

Aurora (Alpha)
    Anzeigen Grotesk (BH)
    Aura (CG)
    Aurora Bold Condensed
    Grotesque Condensed (Dymo)

Aurora (Merg)
    Empira (AI, Alpha, AM, Dymo)
    News No. 2, 8.5 pt., 8 set (CG)
    News No. 12, 8.5 pt., 8 set (CG)
    Polaris
    Regal (HC)
    RG (Itek)

Aurora Bold Condensed
    Anzeigen Grotesk (BH)
    Aura (CG)
    Aurora (Alpha)
    Grotesque Condensed (Dymo)

Aurora Bold Face No. 2 (Merg)
    Boldface No. 2
    News Bold No. 2 (CG)
    News Bold No. 12 (CG)

ITC **Avant Garde Gothic** (AI, Alpha, AM, BH, CG, Dymo, HC, Merg)
    AG (Itek)
    Cadence
    Suave (Wang)

Aztec (AI)
    Aster (BH, CG, Merg)
    Astro (Alpha, Wang)

B

C

Ballardvale (AI, Dymo)
Hanover (AM)
Lyra
Mallard (CG)
ME (Itek)
Medallion (HC)
Melier
Melior (BH, Merg)
Uranus (Alpha)
Ventura (Wang)

Banker's Gothic
Bank Gothic (Dymo, Merg)
Commerce Gothic
De Luxe Gothic (HC)
Stationer's Gothic

Bank Gothic (Dymo, Merg)
Banker's Gothic
Commerce Gothic
De Luxe Gothic (HC)
Stationer's Gothic

Baskerline (Alpha)
Baskerville (AI, AM, BH, CG, Dymo,
HC, IBM, Itek, Merg)
Beaumont (Wang)
BK (Itek)

Baskerville (AI, AM, BH, CG, Dymo,
HC, IBM, Itek, Merg)
Baskerline (Alpha)
Beaumont (Wang)
BK (Itek)

Basque (CG, Dymo)
Sophisticate

Beaumont (Wang)
Baskerline (Alpha)
Baskerville (AI, AM, BH, CG, Dymo,
HC, IBM, Itek, Merg)
BK (Itek)

Bedford (AI, Dymo)
Imperial (HC)
New Bedford (AI)
News No. 4, 8 pt., 8 set (CG)
Taurus

Bem (CG)
Aldine Roman (IBM)
Bembo (AI, AM, BH, Dymo, Merg,
Wang)
Griffo (Alpha)

Bembo (AI, AM, BH, Dymo,
Merg, Wang)
Aldine Roman (IBM)
Bem (CG)
Griffo (Alpha)

Berner (AM)
Sabon (CG, Merg)
Sybil (AI)

Bernhard Cursive
Bridal Script
Liberty (CG, Dymo)
Lotus (HC)

BK (Itek)
Baskerline (Alpha)
Baskerville (AI, AM, BH, CG, Dymo,
HC, IBM, Itek, Merg)
Beaumont (Wang)

BM (Itek)
ITC Bookman (AI, AM, BH, CG,
Merg)

BO (Itek)
Bodoni (AI, Alpha, AM, BH, CG,
Dymo, HC, IBM, Itek, Merg)
Brunswick (Wang)

Bodoni (Alpha, AM, BH, CG, Dymo,
HC, IBM, Itek, Merg)
BO (Itek)
Brunswick (Wang)

Boldface No. 2
Aurora Bold Face No. 2 (Merg)
News Bold No. 2 (CG)
News Bold No. 12 (CG)

Bookface (HC)
Bookman (AI, Alpha, BH, CG, Dymo,
Merg)

Bookman (AI, Alpha, BH, CG, Dymo,
Merg)
Bookface (HC)

ITC **Bookman** (AM, BH, CG, Merg)
BM (Itek)

Boston (Wang)
Alphavers (Alpha)
Aries
Galaxy (HC)
UN (Itek)
Univers (AI, AM, BH, CG, Dymo,
IBM, Merg)
Versatile (Alpha)

Bridal Script
Bernhard Cursive
Liberty (CG, Dymo)
Lotus (HC)

Brunswick (Wang)
BO (Itek)
Bodoni (AI, Alpha, AM, BH, CG,
Dymo, HC, IBM, Itek, Merg)

Cadence
AG (Itek)
ITC Avant Garde Gothic (AI, Alpha,
AM, BH, CG, Dymo, HC, Merg)
Suave (Wang)

Cairo (HC)
Alexandria (Wang)
Memphis (Merg)
Pyramid (IBM)
ST (Itek)
Stymie (AI, Alpha, AM, BH, CG,
Dymo)

Caledo (Alpha)
Caledonia (BH, Merg)
California (CG)
Cornelia
Edinburg (Wang)
Gemini
Highland (AI, Dymo)
Laurel (HC)

Caledonia (BH, Merg)
Caledo (Alpha)
California (CG)
Cornelia
Edinburg (Wang)
Gemini
Highland (AI, Dymo)
Laurel (HC)

California (CG)
Caledo (Alpha)
Caledonia (BH, Merg)
Cornelia
Edinburg (Wang)
Gemini
Highland (AI, Dymo)
Laurel (HC)

Cambridge Expanded (Wang)
CE (Itek)
Century
Century Expanded (AI, Alpha, AM,
BH, Dymo, HC, Merg)
Century Light (CG)
Century X (Alpha)

Cambridge Old Style (Wang)
Century Old Style (Alpha, BH, CG,
HC, Merg)

Cambridge Schoolbook (Wang)
Century Medium (IBM)
Century Modern
Century Schoolbook (AI, BH, Dymo,
Itek, HC, Merg)
Century Text (Alpha)
Century Textbook (CG)
CS (Itek)
Schoolbook

Casual
Ad Bold (AI, Dymo)
Dom Casual (CG)
Polka (BH)

CE (Itek)
Cambridge Expanded (Wang)
Century
Century Expanded (AI, Alpha, AM,
BH, Dymo, HC, Merg)
Century Light (CG)
Century X (Alpha)

Century
Cambridge Expanded (Wang)
CE (Itek)
Century Expanded (AI, Alpha, AM,
BH, Dymo, HC, Merg)
Century Light (CG)
Century X (Alpha)

Century Expanded (AI, Alpha, AM,
BH, Dymo, HC, Merg)
Cambridge Expanded (Wang)
CE (Itek)
Century
Century Light (CG)
Century X (Alpha)

Century Light (CG)
Cambridge Expanded (Wang)
CE (Itek)
Century
Century Expanded (AI, Alpha, AM,
BH, Dymo, HC, Merg)
Century X (Alpha)

Century Medium (IBM)
Cambridge Schoolbook (Wang)
Century Modern
Century Schoolbook (AI, BH, Dymo,
HC, Itek, Merg)
Century Text (Alpha)
Century Textbook (CG)
CS (Itek)
Schoolbook

Century Modern
Cambridge Schoolbook (Wang)
Century Medium (IBM)
Century Schoolbook (AI, BH, Dymo,
HC, Itek, Merg)
Century Text (Alpha)
Century Textbook (CG)
CS (Itek)
Schoolbook

Century Old Style (Alpha, BH, CG, HC,
Merg)
Cambridge Old Style (Wang)

Century Schoolbook (AI, BH, Dymo,
HC, Itek, Merg)
Cambridge Schoolbook (Wang)
Century Medium (IBM)
Century Modern
Century Text (Alpha)
Century Textbook (CG)
CS (Itek)
Schoolbook

Century Text (Alpha)
Cambridge Schoolbook (Wang)
Century Medium (IBM)
Century Modern
Century Schoolbook (AI, BH, Dymo,
HC, Itek, Merg)
Century Textbook (CG)
CS (Itek)
Schoolbook

Century Textbook (CG)
Cambridge Schoolbook (Wang)
Century Medium (IBM)
Century Modern
Century Schoolbook (AI, BH, Dymo,
HC, Itek, Merg)
Century Text (Alpha)
CS (Itek)
Schoolbook

Century X (Alpha)
Cambridge Expanded (Wang)
CE (Itek)
Century
Century Expanded (AI, Alpha, AM,
BH, Dymo, HC, Merg)
Century Light

Chelmsford (AI, AM, Dymo)
Musica (Alpha)
OP (Itek)
Optima (BH, Merg)
Optimist (AI)
Oracle (CG)
Orleans (Wang)
Theme (IBM)
Ursa
Zenith (HC)

Chelsea Black (AI, Dymo)
Gothic No. 3 (CG)
Metro Black (Merg)

Chelsea Light (AI, Dymo)
Gothic No. 2 (CG)
Metrolite (Merg)

Cheltenham (AI, Alpha, AM, BH, CG,
Dymo, Merg)
Cheltonian (HC)
Gloucester
Nordhoff (AI)
Winchester

Cheltonian (HC)
Cheltenham (AI, Alpha, AM, BH, CG,
Dymo, Merg)
Gloucester
Nordhoff (AI)
Winchester

Clarendon (Alpha, AM, BH, CG, Dymo,
Merg)
Clarion (AI)
Clarique (HC)

Clarion (AI)
Clarendon (Alpha, AM, BH, CG,
Dymo, Merg)
Clarique (HC)

Clarique (HC)
Clarendon (Alpha, AM, BH, CG,
Dymo, Merg)
Clarion (AI)

Claro (Alpha)
Corvus
Geneva (AI, Wang)
HE (Itek)
Helios (CG)
Helvetica (BH, Merg)
Megaron (AM)
Newton (AI, Dymo)
Vega (HC)

Classified News Medium (IBM)
Alpha Gothic (Alpha)
News Gothic (AI, Alpha, BH, CG,
Dymo, HC, Wang)
Toledo
Trade Gothic (Merg)

D

Cochin (Merg)
Le Cochin (BH)

Colonial (AM)
Americana (BH, Merg)
American Classic (CG)

Commerce Gothic
Banker's Gothic
Bank Gothic (Dymo, Merg)
De Luxe Gothic (HC)
Stationer's Gothic

Computer (CG)
Moore Computer

Continental (HC)
Knight (Wang)
Mediaeval (AM)
Olympus (Alpha)
Saul (AI)
Trump Imperial
Trump Mediaeval (BH, CG, Merg)

Cooper Black (AI, Alpha, AM, BH, CG, Dymo, Itek)
Pabst (Merg)
Pittsburgh Black

Copper Light
Copperplate (Alpha, BH, CG, Merg)
Copperplate Gothic (BH, Dymo, IBM, Merg)
Formal Gothic (Dymo)
Gothic No. 31 (HC)
Lining Plate Gothic

Copperplate (Alpha, BH, CG, Merg)
Copper Light
Copperplate Gothic (BH, Dymo, IBM, Merg)
Formal Gothic (Dymo)
Gothic No. 31 (HC)
Lining Plate Gothic

Copperplate Gothic (BH, Dymo, IBM, Merg)
Copper Light
Copperplate (Alpha, BH, CG, Merg)
Formal Gothic (Dymo)
Gothic No. 31 (HC)
Lining Plate Gothic

Corinth (AI)
Doric (AI, Dymo)
Ionic (Merg)
News Text Medium (Alpha)

Cornelia
Caledo (Alpha)
Caledonia (BH, Merg)
California (CG)
Edinburg (Wang)
Gemini
Highland (AI, Dymo)
Laurel (HC)

Corona (Merg)
Aquarius
CR (Itek)
Crown (AI, AM, Dymo)
Koronna (Alpha)
News No. 3, 9 pt., 8 set (CG)
News No. 5, 5.5 pt., 6 set (CG)
News No. 6, 8 pt., 8 set (CG)
Nimbus (AI)
Quincy
Royal (HC)
Vela

Corvus
Claro (Alpha)
Geneva (AI, Wang)
HE (Itek)
Helios (CG)
Helvetica (BH, Merg)
Megaron (AM)
Newton (AI, Dymo)
Vega (HC)

CR (Itek)
Aquarius
Corona (Merg)
Crown (AI, AM, Dymo)
Koronna (Alpha)
News No. 3, 9 pt., 8 set (CG)
News No. 5, 5.5 pt., 6 set (CG)
News No. 6, 8 pt., 8 set (CG)
Nimbus (AI)
Quincy
Royal (HC)
Vela

Crown (AI, AM, Dymo)
Aquarius
Corona (Merg)
CR (Itek)
Koronna (Alpha)
News No. 3, 9 pt., 8 set (CG)
News No. 5, 5.5 pt., 6 set (CG)
News No. 6, 8 pt., 8 set (CG)
Nimbus (AI)
Quincy
Royal (HC)
Vela

CS (Itek)
Cambridge Schoolbook (Wang)
Century Medium (IBM)
Century Modern
Century Schoolbook (AI, BH, Dymo, HC, Itek, Merg)
Century Text (Alpha)
Century Textbook (CG)
Schoolbook

De Luxe Gothic (HC)
Banker's Gothic
Bank Gothic (Dymo, Merg)
Commerce Gothic
Stationer's Gothic

Dom Casual (CG)
Ad Bold (AI, Dymo)
Casual
Polka (BH)

Doric (AI, Dymo)
Corinth (AI)
Ionic (Merg)
News Text Medium (Alpha)

Dow News (AI, Dymo)
Ideal (HC)
News No. 9, 8 pt., 8 set (CG)

E

Edelweiss (Alpha)
Weiss (BH, HC, Merg)

Edinburg (Wang)
Caledo (Alpha)
Caledonia (BH, Merg)
California (CG)
Cornelia
Gemini
Highland (AI, Dymo)
Laurel (HC)

Elante (CG)
Electra (Merg)
Selectra (AI)

Electra (Merg)
Elante (CG)
Selectra (AI)

Elegante (HC)
Andover (AI, AM, Dymo)
Malibu (AI)
Paladium (CG)
Palatino (BH, Merg)
Patina (Alpha)
Pontiac (Wang)

Embassy (HC)
Florentine Script (CG)
Helanna Script (AM)
Lucia Script

Empira (AI, Alpha, AM, Dymo)
Aurora (Merg)
News No. 2, 8.5 pt., 8 set (CG)
News No. 12, 8.5 pt., 8 set (CG)
Polaris
Regal (HC)
RG (Itek)

English (Alpha)
English Times (CG)
London Roman (Wang)
Pegasus
Press Roman (IBM)
Times New Roman (BH)
Times Roman (AI, AM, Dymo, HC, Merg)
TR (Itek)

English Times (CG)
English (Alpha)
London Roman (Wang)
Pegasus
Press Roman (IBM)
Times New Roman (BH)
Times Roman (AI, AM, Dymo, HC)
TR (Itek)

ES (Itek)
Eurogothic (Alpha)
Europa (Wang)
Eurostile (AM, BH, Merg)
Eurostyle
Microstyle (CG)
Waltham (Dymo)

Eurogothic (Alpha)
ES (Itek)
Europa (Wang)
Eurostile (AM, BH, Merg)
Eurostyle
Microstyle (CG)
Waltham (Dymo)

Europa (Wang)
ES (Itek)
Eurogothic (Alpha)
Eurostile (AM, BH, Merg)
Eurostyle
Microstyle (CG)
Waltham (Dymo)

Europe
Airport
FU (Itek)
Futura (Alpha, BH, CG, HC, Merg)
Photura (AI, Dymo)
Sirius
Spartan (Merg)
Techno (AI, AM, Dymo)
Tempo
Twentieth Century
Utica (Wang)

Eurostile (AM, BH, Merg)
ES (Itek)
Eurogothic (Alpha)
Europa (Wang)
Eurostyle
Microstyle (CG)
Waltham (Dymo)

Eurostyle
ES (Itek)
Eurogothic (Alpha)
Europa (Wang)
Eurostile (AM, BH, Merg)
Microstyle (CG)
Waltham (Dymo)

Eusebius
Nicholas Jenson

EX (Itek)
Excella (Dymo)
Excelsior (Merg)
News No. 14 (CG)

Excella (Dymo)
EX (Itek)
Excelsior (Merg)
News No. 14 (CG)

Excelsior (Merg)
EX (Itek)
Excella (Dymo)
News No. 14 (CG)

F

Florentine Script (CG)
  Embassy (HC)
  Helanna Script (AM)
  Lucia Script

Floridian Script (CG, Dymo)
  Nuptial

Formal Gothic (Dymo)
  Copper Light
  Copperplate (Alpha, BH, CG, Merg)
  Copperplate Gothic (BH, Dymo,
    IBM, Merg)
  Gothic No. 31 (HC)
  Lining Plate Gothic

Franklin (CG)
  Franklin Gothic (AI, Alpha, AM, BH,
    Dymo, Merg)
  Pittsburgh (Wang)

Franklin Gothic (AI, Alpha, AM, BH,
    Dymo, Merg)
  Franklin (CG)
  Pittsburgh (Wang)

French Script (CG)
  Kaylin Script (AM)

ITC **Friz Quadrata** (AI, Alpha, CG,
    Dymo)
  Katrina (BH)
  Quadrata (Merg)

FU (Itek)
  Airport
  Europe
  Futura (Alpha, BH, CG, HC, Merg)
  Photura (AI, Dymo)
  Sirius
  Spartan (Merg)
  Techno (AI, AM, Dymo)
  Tempo
  Twentieth Century
  Utica (Wang)

Futura (Alpha, BH, CG, HC, Merg)
  Airport
  Europe
  FU (Itek)
  Photura (AI, Dymo)
  Sirius
  Spartan (Merg)
  Techno (AI, AM, Dymo)
  Tempo
  Twentieth Century
  Utica (Wang)

Futura (5.5 pt. Classified Ad) (HC)
  Sans 5.5 pt., 6 set (CG)
  Spartan (Merg)
  Techno Book (AI, AM, Dymo)
  Utica Book (Wang)

G

Galaxy (HC)
  Alphavers (Alpha)
  Aries
  Boston (Wang)
  UN (Itek)
  Univers (AI, AM, BH, CG, Dymo,
    IBM, Merg)
  Versatile (Alpha)

Garamond (AI, Alpha, AM, CG, BH,
    Dymo, HC, Merg)
  GD (Itek)
  Grenada (Wang)

GD (Itek)
  Garamond (AI, Alpha, AM, BH, CG,
    Dymo, HC, Merg)
  Grenada (Wang)

Gemini
  Caledo (Alpha)
  Caledonia (BH, Merg)
  California (CG)
  Cornelia
  Edinburg (Wang)
  Highland (AI, Dymo)
  Laurel (HC)

Geneva (AI, Wang)
  Claro (Alpha)
  Corvus
  HE (Itek)
  Helios (CG)
  Helvetica (BH, Merg)
  Megaron (AM)
  Newton (AI, Dymo)
  Vega (HC)

Gill Sans (BH, CG, Merg)
  Glib (Alpha)
  Graphic Gothic (Wang)

Glib (Alpha)
  Gill Sans (BH, CG, Merg)
  Graphic Gothic (Wang)

Gloucester
  Cheltenham (AI, Alpha, AM, BH,
    CG, Dymo, Merg)
  Cheltonian (HC)
  Nordhoff (AI)
  Winchester

Gold Nugget (CG)
  Gold Rush (BH)
  Klondike

Gold Rush (BH)
  Gold Nugget (CG)
  Klondike

Gothic No. 1 (CG)
  Gothic 19 (Merg)

Gothic No. 2 (CG)
  Chelsea Light (AI, Dymo)
  Metrolite (Merg)

Gothic No. 3 (CG)
  Chelsea Black (AI, Dymo)
  Metro Black (Merg)

Gothic No. 4 (CG)
  Gothic 13 (Merg)

Gothic 13 (AI, Merg)
  Gothic No. 4 (CG)

Gothic 19 (Merg)
  Gothic No. 1 (CG)

Gothic No. 31 (HC)
  Copper Light
  Copperplate (Alpha, BH, CG, Merg)
  Copperplate Gothic (BH, Dymo, IBM,
    Merg)
  Formal Gothic (Dymo)
  Lining Plate Gothic

Goudy Light (Dymo)
  Goudy Old Style (Alpha, BH, CG, HC,
    Merg)
  Grecian (Wang)
  Number 11

Goudy Old Style (AI, Alpha, BH, CG, HC,
    Merg)
  Goudy Light (Dymo)
  Grecian (Wang)
  Number 11

Granite (AI, Dymo)
  Lisbon (CG)
  Lydian (BH, HC)

Graphic Gothic (Wang)
  Gill Sans (BH, CG, Merg)
  Glib (Alpha)

Grecian (Wang)
  Goudy Light (Dymo)
  Goudy Old Style (AI, Alpha, BH, CG,
    HC, Merg)
  Number 11

Grenada (Wang)
    Garamond (AI, Alpha, AM, BH,
      CG, Dymo, HC, Merg)
    GD (Itek)

Griffo (Alpha)
    Aldine Roman (IBM)
    Bem (CG)
    Bembo (AI, AM, BH, Dymo,
      Merg, Wang)

Grotesque Condensed (Dymo)
    Anzeigen Grotesk (BH)
    Aura (CG)
    Aurora (Alpha)
    Aurora Bold Condensed

Hanover (AM)
    Ballardvale (AI, Dymo)
    Lyra
    Mallard (CG)
    ME (Itek)
    Medallion (HC)
    Melier
    Melior (BH, Merg)
    Uranus (Alpha)
    Ventura (Wang)

HE (Itek)
    Claro (Alpha)
    Corvus
    Geneva (AI, Wang)
    Helios (CG)
    Helvetica (BH, Merg)
    Megaron (AM)
    Newton (AI, Dymo)
    Vega (HC)

Helanna Script (AM)
    Embassy (HC)
    Florentine Script (CG)
    Lucia Script

Helios (CG)
    Claro (Alpha)
    Corvus
    Geneva (AI, Wang)
    HE (Itek)
    Helvetica (BH, Merg)
    Megaron (AM)
    Newton (AI, Dymo)
    Vega (HC)

Helvetica (BH, Merg)
    Claro (Alpha)
    Corvus
    Geneva (AI, Wang)
    HE (Itek)
    Helios (CG)
    Megaron (AM)
    Newton (AI, Dymo)
    Vega (HC)

Highland (AI, Dymo)
    Caledo (Alpha)
    Caledonia (BH, Merg)
    California (CG)
    Cornelia
    Edinburg (Wang)
    Gemini
    Laurel (HC)

Hobo (BH, Merg)
    Tramp (AI)

Ideal (HC)
    Dow News (AI, Dymo)
    News No. 9, 8 pt., 8 set (CG)

Imperial (HC)
    Bedford (AI, Dymo)
    New Bedford (AI)
    News No. 4, 8 pt., 8 set (CG)
    Taurus

Ionic (Merg)
    Corinth (AI)
    Doric (AI, Dymo)
    News Text Medium (Alpha)

J   K   L

Jenny
  Souvenir Gothic (Alpha, CG)

Jewel (Wang)
  ITC Tiffany (AI, Alpha, AM, BH,
    CG, Dymo, Merg)

ITC **Kabel** (Alpha, AM, BH, CG, Merg)
  Kabot (Wang)
  Sans Serif

Kabot (Wang)
  ITC Kabel (Alpha, AM, BH, CG,
    Merg)
  Sans Serif

Katrina (BH)
  ITC Friz Quadrata (AI, Alpha, CG,
    Dymo)
  Quadrata (Merg)

Kaylin Script (AM)
  French Script (CG)

Kennerley (CG)
  Kenntonian (HC)
  Kensington (AI)
  LSE Kennerley

Kenntonian (HC)
  Kennerley (CG)
  Kensington (AI)
  LSE Kennerley

Kensington (AI)
  Kennerley (CG)
  Kenntonian (HC)
  LSE Kennerley

Klondike
  Gold Nugget (CG)
  Gold Rush (BH)

Knight
  Continental (HC)
  Mediaeval (AM)
  Olympus (Alpha)
  Saul (AI)
  Trump Imperial
  Trump Mediaeval (BH, CG, Merg)

Kordova (Wang)
  ITC Korinna (AI, Alpha, AM, BH,
    CG, Dymo, Merg)

ITC **Korinna** (AI, Alpha, AM, BH,
    CG, Dymo, Merg)
  Kordova (Wang)

Koronna (Alpha)
  Aquarius
  Corona (Merg)
  CR (Itek)
  Crown (AI, AM, Dymo)
  News No. 3, 9 pt., 8 set (CG)
  News No. 5, 5.5 pt., 6 set (CG)
  News No. 6, 8 pt., 8 set (CG)
  Nimbus (AI)
  Quincy
  Royal (HC)
  Vela

Latine (AI, Dymo)
  Meridien (BH, Dymo, Merg)
  Zenith (Wang)

Laurel (HC)
  Caledo (Alpha)
  Caledonia (BH, Merg)
  California (CG)
  Cornelia
  Edinburg (Wang)
  Gemini
  Highland (AI, Dymo)

Le Cochin (BH)
  Cochin (Merg)

Liberty (CG, Dymo)
  Bernhard Cursive
  Bridal Script
  Lotus (HC)

Libra (CG)
  Libretto (Alpha)

Libretto (Alpha)
  Libra (CG)

Line Gothic (Wang)
  ITC Serif Gothic (AI, Alpha, AM, BH,
    CG, Dymo, Merg)

Lining Plate Gothic
  Copper Light
  Copperplate (Alpha, BH, CG, Merg)
  Copperplate Gothic (BH, Dymo, IBM,
    Merg)
  Formal Gothic (Dymo)
  Gothic No. 31 (HC)

Lisbon (CG)
  Granite (AI, Dymo)
  Lydian (BH, HC)

M

London Roman (Wang)
English (Alpha)
English Times (CG)
Pegasus
Press Roman (IBM)
Times New Roman (BH)
Times Roman (AI, AM, Dymo,
HC, Merg)
TR (Itek)

Lorraine (AI, Dymo)
Venetian Script (CG)

Lotus (HC)
Bernhard Cursive
Bridal Script
Liberty (CG, Dymo)

LSE Kennerley
Kennerley (CG)
Kenntonian (HC)
Kensington (AI)

Lucia Script
Embassy (HC)
Florentine Script (CG)
Helanna Script (AM)

Lydian (BH, HC)
Granite (AI, Dymo)
Lisbon (CG)

Lyra
Ballardvale (AI, Dymo)
Hanover (AM)
Mallard (CG)
ME (Itek)
Medallion (HC)
Melier
Melior (BH, Merg)
Uranus (Alpha)
Ventura (Wang)

Malibu (AI)
Andover (AI, AM, Dymo)
Elegante (HC)
Paladium (CG)
Palatino (BH, Merg)
Patina (Alpha)
Pontiac (Wang)

Mallard (CG)
Ballardvale (AI, Dymo)
Hanover (AM)
Lyra
ME (Itek)
Medallion (HC)
Melier
Melior (BH, Merg)
Uranus (Alpha)
Ventura (Wang)

ME (Itek)
Ballardvale (AI, Dymo)
Hanover (AM)
Lyra
Mallard (CG)
Medallion (HC)
Melier
Melior (BH, Merg)
Uranus (Alpha)
Ventura (Wang)

Medallion (HC)
Ballardvale (AI, Dymo)
Hanover (AM)
Lyra
Mallard (CG)
ME (Itek)
Melier
Melior (BH, Merg)
Uranus (Alpha)
Ventura (Wang)

Mediaeval (AM)
Continental (HC)
Knight (Wang)
Olympus (Alpha)
Saul (AI)
Trump Imperial
Trump Mediaeval (BH, CG, Merg)

Megaron (AM)
Claro (Alpha)
Corvus
Geneva (AI, Wang)
HE (Itek)
Helios (CG)
Helvetica (BH, Merg)
Newton (AI, Dymo)
Vega (HC)

Melier
Ballardvale (AI, Dymo)
Hanover (AM)
Lyra
Mallard (CG)
ME (Itek)
Medallion (HC)
Melior (BH, Merg)
Uranus (Alpha)
Ventura (Wang)

Melior (BH, Merg)
Ballardvale (AI, Dymo)
Hanover (AM)
Lyra
Mallard (CG)
ME (Itek)
Medallion (HC)
Melier
Uranus (Alpha)
Ventura (Wang)

Memphis (Merg)
Alexandria (Wang)
Cairo (HC)
Pyramid (IBM)
ST (Itek)
Stymie (AI, Alpha, AM, BH, CG,
Dymo)

Meridien (BH, Dymo, Merg)
Latine (AI, Dymo)
Zenith (Wang)

Metro Black (Merg)
Chelsea Black (AI, Dymo)
Gothic No. 3 (CG)

Metrolite (Merg)
Chelsea Light (AI, Dymo)
Gothic No. 2 (CG)

Microstyle (CG)
ES (Itek)
Eurogothic (Alpha)
Europa (Wang)
Eurostile (AM, BH, Merg)
Eurostyle
Waltham (Dymo)

N

Minuet (HC)
Piranesi (CG, Dymo)

Moore Computer
Computer (CG)

Musica (Alpha)
Chelmsford (AI, AM, Dymo)
OP (Itek)
Optima (BH, Merg)
Optimist (AI)
Oracle (CG)
Orleans (Wang)
Theme (IBM)
Ursa
Zenith (HC)

New Bedford (AI)
Bedford (AI, Dymo)
Imperial (HC)
News No. 4, 8 pt., 8 set (CG)
Taurus

News Gothic (AI, Alpha, BH, CG, Dymo, HC, Wang)
Alpha Gothic (Alpha)
Classified News Medium (IBM)
Toledo
Trade Gothic (Merg)

News No. 2, 8.5 pt., 8 set (CG)
Aurora (Merg)
Empira (Alpha, AM, Dymo)
News No. 12, 8.5 pt., 8 set (CG)
Polaris
Regal (HC)
RG (Itek)

News Bold No. 2 (CG)
Aurora Bold Face No. 2 (Merg)
Boldface No. 2
News Bold No. 12 (CG)

News No. 3, 9 pt., 8 set (CG)
Aquarius
Corona (Merg)
CR (Itek)
Crown (AI, AM, Dymo)
Koronna (Alpha)
News No. 5, 5.5 pt., 6 set (CG)
News No. 6, 8 pt., 8 set (CG)
Nimbus (AI)
Quincy
Royal (HC)
Vela

News No. 4, 8 pt., 8 set (CG)
Bedford (AI, Dymo)
Imperial (HC)
New Bedford (AI)
Taurus

News No. 5, 5.5 pt., 6 set (CG)
Aquarius
Corona (Merg)
CR (Itek)
Crown (AI, AM, Dymo)
Koronna (Alpha)
News No. 3, 9 pt., 8 set (CG)
News No. 6, 8 pt., 8 set (CG)
Nimbus (AI)
Quincy
Royal (HC)
Vela

News No. 6, 8 pt., 8 set (CG)
Aquarius
Corona (Merg)
CR (Itek)
Crown (AI, AM, Dymo)
Koronna (Alpha)
News No. 3, 9 pt., 8 set (CG)
News No. 5, 5.5 pt., 6 set (CG)
Nimbus (AI)
Quincy
Royal (HC)
Vela

News No. 9, 8 pt., 8 set (CG)
Dow News (AI, Dymo)
Ideal (HC)

News No. 10, 10 pt., 9.5 set (CG)
Rex (Merg)
Zar (Dymo)

News No. 12, 8.5 pt., 8 set (CG)
Aurora (Merg)
Empira (AI, Alpha, AM, Dymo)
News No. 2, 8.5 pt., 8 set (CG)
Polaris
Regal (HC)
RG (Itek)

News Bold No. 12 (CG)
Aurora Bold Face No. 2 (Merg)
Bold Face No. 2
News Bold No. 2 (CG)

News No. 14 (CG)
EX (Itek)
Excella (Dymo)
Excelsior (Merg)

News Text Medium (Alpha)
Corinth (AI)
Doric (AI, Dymo)
Ionic (Merg)

O

Newton (AI, Dymo)
  Claro (Alpha)
  Corvus
  Geneva (AI, Wang)
  HE (Itek)
  Helios (CG)
  Helvetica (BH, Merg)
  Megaron (AM)
  Vega (HC)

Nicholas Jenson
  Eusebius

Nimbus (AI)
  Aquarius
  Corona (Merg)
  CR (Itek)
  Crown (AI, Dymo, Merg)
  Koronna (Alpha)
  News No. 3, 9 pt., 8 set (CG)
  News No. 5, 5.5 pt., 6 set (CG)
  News No. 6, 8 pt., 8 set (CG)
  Quincy
  Royal (HC)
  Vela

Nordhoff (AI)
  Cheltenham (AI, Alpha, AM, BH,
    CG, Dymo, Merg)
  Cheltonian (HC)
  Gloucester
  Winchester

Number 11
  Goudy Light (Dymo)
  Goudy Old Style (AI, Alpha, BH,
    CG, HC, Merg)
  Grecian (Wang)

Nuptial
  Floridian Script (CG, Dymo)

Oliva
  Antique Olive (BH, CG, Merg)
  Olive (AM)
  Olivette
  Olivette Antique (Wang)

Olive (AM)
  Antique Olive (BH, CG, Merg)
  Oliva
  Olivette
  Olivette Antique (Wang)

Olivette
  Antique Olive (BH, CG, Merg)
  Oliva
  Olive (AM)
  Olivette Antique (Wang)

Olivette Antique (Wang)
  Antique Olive (BH, CG, Merg)
  Oliva
  Olive (AM)
  Olivette

Olympus (Alpha)
  Continental (HC)
  Knight (Wang)
  Mediaeval (AM)
  Saul (AI)
  Trump Imperial
  Trump Mediaeval (BH, CG, Merg)

OP (Itek)
  Chelmsford (AI, AM, Dymo)
  Musica (Alpha)
  Optima (BH, Merg)
  Optimist (AI)
  Oracle (CG)
  Orleans (Wang)
  Theme (IBM)
  Ursa
  Zenith (HC)

Optima (BH, Merg)
  Chelmsford (AI, AM, Dymo)
  Musica (Alpha)
  OP (Itek)
  Optimist (AI)
  Oracle (CG)
  Orleans (Wang)
  Theme (IBM)
  Ursa
  Zenith (HC)

Optimist (AI)
  Chelmsford (AI, AM, Dymo)
  Musica (Alpha)
  OP (Itek)
  Optima (BH, Merg)
  Oracle (CG)
  Orleans (Wang)
  Theme (IBM)
  Ursa
  Zenith (HC)

Oracle (CG)
  Chelmsford (AI, AM, Dymo)
  Musica (Alpha)
  OP (Itek)
  Optima (BH, Merg)
  Optimist (AI)
  Orleans (Wang)
  Theme (IBM)
  Ursa
  Zenith (HC)

Original Script (CG)
  Typo Script

Orleans (Wang)
  Chelmsford (AI, AM, Dymo)
  Musica (Alpha)
  OP (Itek)
  Optima (BH, Merg)
  Optimist (AI)
  Oracle (CG)
  Theme (IBM)
  Ursa
  Zenith (HC)

P

PA (Itek)
    Park Avenue (AM, CG, Dymo, HC, Merg)

Pabst (Merg)
    Cooper Black (AI, Alpha, AM, BH, CG, Dymo, Itek)
    Pittsburgh Black

Paladium (CG)
    Andover (AI, AM, Dymo)
    Elegante (HC)
    Malibu (AI)
    Palatino (BH, Merg)
    Patina (Alpha)
    Pontiac (Wang)

Palatino (BH, Merg)
    Andover (AI, AM, Dymo)
    Elegante (HC)
    Malibu (AI)
    Paladium (CG)
    Patina (Alpha)
    Pontiac (Wang)

Park Avenue (AM, CG, Dymo, HC, Merg)
    PA (Itek)

Patina (Alpha)
    Andover (AI, AM, Dymo)
    Elegante (HC)
    Malibu (AI)
    Paladium (CG)
    Palatino (BH, Merg)
    Pontiac (Wang)

Pegasus
    English (Alpha)
    English Times (CG)
    London Roman (Wang)
    Press Roman (IBM)
    Times New Roman (BH)
    Times Roman (AI, AM, Dymo, HC, Merg)
    TR (Itek)

Peignot (BH, Merg)
    Penyoe (CG)

Penyoe (CG)
    Peignot (BH, Merg)

Percepta (Alpha)
    Perpetua (AI, AM, BH, CG, Dymo)
    Perpetual (Wang)

Perpetua (AI, AM, BH, CG, Dymo)
    Percepta (Alpha)
    Perpetual (Wang)

Perpetual (Wang)
    Percepta (Alpha)
    Perpetua (AI, AM, BH, CG, Dymo)

Photura (AI, Dymo)
    Airport
    Europe
    FU (Itek)
    Futura (Alpha, BH, CG, HC, Merg)
    Sirius
    Spartan (Merg)
    Techno (AI, AM, Dymo)
    Tempo
    Twentieth Century
    Utica (Wang)

Piranesi (CG, Dymo)
    Minuet (HC)

Pittsburgh (Wang)
    Franklin (CG)
    Franklin Gothic (AI, Alpha, AM, BH, Dymo, Merg)

Pittsburgh Black
    Cooper Black (AI, Alpha, AM, BH, CG, Dymo, Itek)
    Pabst (Merg)

PL (Itek)
    Atlantic (Alpha)
    Planet (Wang)
    Plantin (AI, AM, BH, CG, Dymo, Merg)

Planet (Wang)
    Atlantic (Alpha)
    PL (Itek)
    Plantin (AI, AM, BH, CG, Dymo, Merg)

Plantin (AI, AM, BH, CG, Dymo, Merg)
    Atlantic (Alpha)
    PL (Itek)
    Planet (Wang)

Polaris
    Aurora (Merg)
    Empira (AI, Alpha, AM, Dymo)
    News No. 2, 8.5 pt., 8 set (CG)
    News No. 12, 8.5 pt., 8 set (CG)
    Regal (HC)
    RG (Itek)

Polka (BH)
    Ad Bold (AI, Dymo)
    Casual
    Dom Casual (CG)

Pontiac (Wang)
    Andover (AI, AM, Dymo)
    Elegante (HC)
    Malibu (AI)
    Paladium (CG)
    Palatino (BH, Merg)
    Patina (Alpha)

Premier (AI)
    Primer (Merg)
    Rector (Alpha)

Press Roman (IBM)
    English (Alpha)
    English Times (CG)
    London Roman (Wang)
    Pegasus
    Times New Roman (BH)
    Times Roman (AI, AM, Dymo, HC, Merg)
    TR (Itek)

Primer (Merg)
    Premier (AI)
    Rector (Alpha)

Pyramid (IBM)
    Alexandria (Wang)
    Cairo (HC)
    Memphis (Merg)
    ST (Itek)
    Stymie (AI, Alpha, AM, BH, CG, Dymo)

Q   R   S

QS (Itek)
  Quill (CG)
  Thompson Quill Script

Quadrata (Merg)
  ITC Friz Quadrata (AI, Alpha,
    CG, Dymo)
  Katrina (BH)

Quill (CG)
  QS (Itek)
  Thompson Quill Script

Quincy
  Aquarius
  Corona (Merg)
  CR (Itek)
  Crown (AI, AM, Dymo)
  Koronna (Alpha)
  News No. 3, 9 pt., 8 set (CG)
  News No. 5, 5.5 pt., 6 set (CG)
  News No. 6, 8 pt., 8 set (CG)
  Nimbus (AI)
  Royal (HC)
  Vela

Rector (Alpha)
  Premier (AI)
  Primer (Merg)

Regal (HC)
  Aurora (Merg)
  Empira (AI, Alpha, AM, Dymo)
  News No. 2, 8.5 pt., 8 set (CG)
  News No. 12, 8.5 pt., 8 set (CG)
  Polaris
  RG (Itek)

Rex (Merg)
  News No. 10, 10 pt., 9.5 set (CG)
  Zar (Dymo)

RG (Itek)
  Aurora (Merg)
  Empira (AI, Alpha, AM, Dymo)
  News No. 2, 8.5 pt., 8 set (CG)
  News No. 12, 8.5 pt., 8 set (CG)
  Polaris
  Regal (HC)

Roman Stylus (CG, Dymo)
  Typo Roman Shaded

Royal (HC)
  Aquarius
  Corona (Merg)
  CR (Itek)
  Crown (AI, AM, Dymo)
  Koronna (Alpha)
  News No. 3, 9 pt., 8 set (CG)
  News No. 5, 5.5 pt., 6 set (CG)
  News No. 6, 8 pt., 8 set (CG)
  Nimbus (AI)
  Quincy
  Vela

Sabon (CG, Merg)
  Berner (AM)
  Sybil (AI)

Sans 5.5 pt., 6 set (CG)
  Futura (HC)
  Spartan (Merg)
  Techno Book (AI, AM, Dymo)
  Utica Book (Wang)

Sans Serif
  ITC Kabel (Alpha, AM, CG, BH,
    Merg)
  Kabot (Wang)

Saul (AI)
  Continental (HC)
  Knight (Wang)
  Mediaeval (AM)
  Olympus (Alpha)
  Trump Imperial
  Trump Mediaeval (BH, CG, Merg)

Schoolbook
  Cambridge Schoolbook (Wang)
  Century Medium (IBM)
  Century Modern
  Century Schoolbook (AI, BH, Dymo,
    HC, Itek, Merg)
  Century Text (Alpha)
  Century Textbook (CG)
  CS (Itek)

Selectra (AI)
  Elante (CG)
  Electra (Merg)

ITC **Serif Gothic** (AI, Alpha, AM, BH, CG,
    Dymo, Merg)
  Line Gothic (Wang)

Sirius
  Airport
  Europe
  FU (Itek)
  Futura (Alpha, BH, CG, HC, Merg)
  Photura (AI, Dymo)
  Spartan (Merg)
  Techno (AI, AM, Dymo)
  Tempo
  Twentieth Century
  Utica (Wang)

Society Text
  Wedding Text (AM, BH)

Sophisticate
  Basque (CG, Dymo)

ITC **Souvenir** (AI, Alpha, AM, BH, CG,
    Dymo, HC, Merg)
  Sovran (Wang)
  SV (Itek)

T

Souvenir Gothic (Alpha, CG)
  Jenny

Sovran (Wang)
  ITC Souvenir (AI, Alpha, AM, BH,
    CG, Dymo, HC, Merg)
  SV (Itek)

Spartan (Merg)
  Airport
  Europe
  FU (Itek)
  Futura (Alpha, BH, CG, HC, Merg)
  Photura (AI, Dymo)
  Sirius
  Techno (AI, AM, Dymo)
  Tempo
  Twentieth Century
  Utica (Wang)

Spartan (5.5 pt. Classified Ad) (Merg)
  Futura (HC)
  Sans 5.5 pt., 6 set (CG)
  Techno Book (AI, AM, Dymo)
  Utica Book (Wang)

ST (Itek)
  Alexandria (Wang)
  Cairo (HC)
  Memphis (Merg)
  Pyramid (IBM)
  Stymie (AI, Alpha, AM, BH, CG,
    Dymo)

Stationer's Gothic
  Banker's Gothic
  Bank Gothic (Dymo, Merg)
  Commerce Gothic
  De Luxe Gothic (HC)

Stylon (AI, Dymo)
  Vogue

Stymie (AI, Alpha, AM, BH, CG, Dymo)
  Alexandria (Wang)
  Cairo (HC)
  Memphis (Merg)
  Pyramid (IBM)
  ST (Itek)

Suave (Wang)
  AG (Itek)
  ITC Avant Garde Gothic (AI, Alpha,
    AM, BH, CG, Dymo, HC, Merg)
  Cadence

SV (Itek)
  ITC Souvenir (AI, Alpha, AM, BH,
    CG, Dymo, HC, Merg)
  Sovran (Wang)

Sybil (AI)
  Berner (AM)
  Sabon (CG, Merg)

Taurus
  Bedford (AI, Dymo)
  Imperial (HC)
  New Bedford (AI)
  News No. 4, 8 pt., 8 set (CG)

Techno (AI, AM, Dymo)
  Airport
  Europe
  FU (Itek)
  Futura (Alpha, BH, CG, HC, Merg)
  Photura (AI, Dymo)
  Sirius
  Spartan (Merg)
  Tempo
  Twentieth Century
  Utica (Wang)

Techno Book (AI, AM, Dymo)
  Futura (HC)
  Sans 5.5 pt., 6 set (CG)
  Spartan (Merg)
  Utica Book (Wang)

Tempo
  Airport
  Europe
  FU (Itek)
  Futura (Alpha, BH, CG, HC, Merg)
  Photura (AI, Dymo)
  Sirius
  Spartan (Merg)
  Techno (AI, AM, Dymo)
  Twentieth Century
  Utica (Wang)

Theme (IBM)
  Chelmsford (AI, AM, Dymo)
  Musica (Alpha)
  OP (Itek)
  Optima (BH, Merg)
  Optimist (AI)
  Oracle (CG)
  Orleans (Wang)
  Ursa
  Zenith (HC)

Thompson Quill Script
  QS (Itek)
  Quill (CG)

ITC **Tiffany** (AI, Alpha, AM, BH, CG,
  Dymo, Merg)
  Jewel (Wang)

Times New Roman (BH)
  English (Alpha)
  English Times (CG)
  London Roman (Wang)
  Pegasus
  Press Roman (IBM)
  Times Roman (AI, AM, Dymo, HC,
    Merg)
  TR (Itek)

Times Roman (AI, AM, Dymo, HC, Merg)
  English (Alpha)
  English Times (CG)
  London Roman (Wang)
  Pegasus
  Press Roman (IBM)
  Times New Roman (BH)
  TR (Itek)

Toledo
  Alpha Gothic (Alpha)
  Classified News Medium (IBM)
  News Gothic (AI, Alpha, BH, CG,
    Dymo, HC, Wang)
  Trade Gothic (Merg)

TR (Itek)
  English (Alpha)
  English Times (CG)
  London Roman (Wang)
  Pegasus
  Press Roman (IBM)
  Times New Roman (BH)
  Times Roman (AI, AM, Dymo, HC,
    Merg)

Trade Gothic (Merg)
  Alpha Gothic (Alpha)
  Classified News Medium (IBM)
  News Gothic (AI, Alpha, BH, CG,
    Dymo, HC, Wang)
  Toledo

Tramp (AI)
  Hobo (BH, Merg)

Trump Imperial
  Continental (HC)
  Knight (Wang)
  Mediaeval (AM)
  Olympus (Alpha)
  Saul (AI)
  Trump Mediaeval (BH, CG, Merg)

U

Trump Mediaeval (BH, CG, Merg)
Continental (HC)
Knight (Wang)
Mediaeval (AM)
Olympus (Alpha)
Saul (AI)
Trump Imperial

Twentieth Century
Airport
Europe
FU (Itek)
Futura (Alpha, BH, CG, HC, Merg)
Photura (AI, Dymo)
Sirius
Spartan (Merg)
Techno (AI, AM, Dymo)
Tempo
Utica (Wang)

Typo Roman Shaded
Roman Stylus (CG, Dymo)

Typo Script
Original Script (CG)

UN (Itek)
Alphavers (Alpha)
Aries
Boston (Wang)
Galaxy (HC)
Univers (AI, AM, BH, CG, Dymo, IBM, Merg)
Versatile (Alpha)

Uncial (CG)
American Uncial (BH)

Uncle Bill (BH)
Uncle Sam Open (CG)

Uncle Sam Open (CG)
Uncle Bill (BH)

Univers (AI, AM, BH, CG, Dymo, IBM, Merg)
Alphavers (Alpha)
Aries
Boston (Wang)
Galaxy (HC)
UN (Itek)
Versatile (Alpha)

Uranus (Alpha)
Ballardvale (AI, Dymo)
Hanover (AM)
Lyra
Mallard (CG)
ME (Itek)
Medallion (HC)
Melier
Melior (BH, Merg)
Ventura (Wang)

Ursa
Chelmsford (AI, AM, Dymo)
Musica (Alpha)
OP (Itek)
Optima (BH, Merg)
Optimist (AI)
Oracle (CG)
Orleans (Wang)
Theme (IBM)
Zenith (HC)

Utica (Wang)
Airport
Europe
FU (Itek)
Futura (Alpha, BH, CG, HC, Merg)
Photura (AI, Dymo)
Sirius
Spartan (Merg)
Techno (AI, AM, Dymo)
Tempo
Twentieth Century

Utica Book (Wang)
Futura (HC)
Sans 5.5 pt., 6 set (CG)
Spartan (Merg)
Techno Book (AI, AM, Dymo)

V   W   Z

Vega (HC)
    Claro (Alpha)
    Corvus
    Geneva (AI, Wang)
    HE (Itek)
    Helios (CG)
    Helvetica (BH, Merg)
    Megaron (AM)
    Newton (AI, Dymo)

Vela
    Aquarius
    Corona (Merg)
    CR (Itek)
    Crown (AI, AM, Dymo)
    Koronna (Alpha)
    News No. 3, 9 pt., 8 set (CG)
    News No. 5, 5.5 pt., 6 set (CG)
    News No. 6, 8 pt., 8 set (CG)
    Nimbus (AI)
    Quincy
    Royal (HC)

Venetian Script (CG)
    Lorraine (AI, Dymo)

Ventura (Wang)
    Ballardvale (AI, Dymo)
    Hanover (AM)
    Lyra
    Mallard (CG)
    ME (Itek)
    Medallion (HC)
    Melier
    Melior (BH, Merg)
    Uranus (Alpha)

Versatile (Alpha)
    Alphavers (Alpha)
    Aries
    Boston (Wang)
    Galaxy (HC)
    UN (Itek)
    Univers (AI, AM, BH, CG, Dymo,
      IBM, Merg)

Vogue
    Stylon (AI, Dymo)

Waltham (Dymo)
    ES (Itek)
    Eurogothic (Alpha)
    Europa (Wang)
    Eurostile (AM, BH, Merg)
    Eurostyle
    Microstyle (CG)

Wedding Text (AM, BH)
    Society Text

Weiss (BH, HC, Merg)
    Edelweiss (Alpha)

Winchester
    Cheltenham (AI, Alpha, AM, BH,
      CG, Dymo, Merg)
    Cheltonian (HC)
    Gloucester
    Nordhoff (AI)

Windsor (AI, BH, CG, Merg)
    Winslow (Alpha)

Winslow (Alpha)
    Windsor (AI, BH, CG, Merg)

ITC **Zapf Book** (AI, AM, BH, CG, Merg)
    ZF (Itek)

Zar (Dymo)
    News No. 10, 10 pt., 9.5 set (CG)
    Rex (Merg)

Zenith (HC)
    Chelmsford (AI, AM, Dymo)
    Musica (Alpha)
    OP (Itek)
    Optima (BH, Merg)
    Optimist (AI)
    Oracle (CG)
    Orleans (Wang)
    Theme (IBM)
    Ursa

Zenith (Wang)
    Latine (AI, Dymo)
    Meridien (BH, Dymo, Merg)

ZF (Itek)
    ITC Zapf Book (AI, AM, BH, CG,
      Merg)

Glossary

Alternate Character: A character within the same font that differs from the standard design. Usually used to add distinction to headlines and display composition.

Ampersand: Contraction of "and." An evolvement from the latin ligature *et.*

Arm: A horizontal stroke that is free on one or both ends.

Ascender: The part of the lowercase letters "b," "d," "f," "h," "k," "l," and "t" that extends above the x-height.

Bar: The horizontal stroke of the "e," "f," "t," "A," "H," and "T."

Baseline: An imaginary line on which the capital letters rest.

Black Letter: Type based on medieval script. A classic example is Old English.

Bowl: A curved stroke that encloses a counter.

Calligraphy: A writing style based on flat-tipped pen or brush strokes.

Cap-line: An imaginary line that runs along the top of the capital letters.

Condensed: Classification of a typestyle in which the letters are narrower than normal.

Counter: Fully or partially enclosed space within a letter.

Cursive: Resembling handwritten script.

Descender: The part of the letters "g," "j," "p," "q," "y," "J," and "Q," that extends below the baseline.

Ear: The small stroke projecting from the right side of the upper bowl of the lowercase "g."

Em: Normally the square of the point size of type used. Can be narrower, or wider, depending on the proportions of the typestyle.

En: Half the width of an em.

Expanded: Classification of a typestyle in which the letters are wider than normal.

Font: A range of letters within a particular typestyle.

Fraktur: The German name given to black letter typestyles.

Gothic: Sometimes referring to black letter, or Fraktur types; but in the United States to sans serif designs.

Grotesque: Sometimes referring to sans serif design.

Hairline: The thin strokes in a serif type design.

Hot Metal Type: Type used for letterpress printing.

Italic: Type in which the letters are obliqued. Cursive typestyles are normally italic, but not all italics are cursive.

Justified Composition: Lines of copy that are flush on the left and right edges.

Kern: To space two letters closer together than customary, to create consistent spacing between all letters.

Leading: See "Line Space." Refers to the thin strips of lead placed between lines of metal type to increase line space.

Leg: The bottom diagonal on the uppercase and lowercase "k."

Ligature: Two or more characters linked together.

Line Space: Extra white space inserted between lines of composition. Previously referred to as leading.

Link: A stroke connecting the upper bowl and lower loop of the lowercase "g."

Logotype: Two or more characters designed as a total entity.

Loop: The lower portion of the lowercase "g."

Lowercase: Small letters. The name is derived from hand composition of metal type. When type was set by hand two cases were used to hold the individual metal type, with one case arranged higher than the other. The capitals were kept in the "uppercase" and the small letters in the "lowercase."

Measure: The length of line to which type is set.

Mutton: Metal typesetting slang for an em.

Nut: Metal typesetting slang for an en.

Oldstyle Numbers: Numbers with ascenders and descenders.

Pi Characters: Characters contained within a font that are not typeface sensitive. Usually reference marks.

Pica: A measure of type equal to 12 points or approximately ⅙ of an inch. Derived from an old term for metal type of the same size.

Point: Smallest increment of typographic measurement, equal to 0.0138 inch. Twelve points equal a pica.

Roman: Name often applied to the Latin alphabet as it is used in English and European languages. Also used to identify upright, as opposed to italic or cursive, alphabet designs.

Sans Serif: Letters without serifs.

Script: Type designed after handwriting or writing with a brush.

Serif: A line crossing the main strokes of a character. It may take on many varieties.

Shoulder: The curved stroke emitting from a stem.

Small Caps: Letters the approximate size of lowercase characters, but the design of the capitals. Normally only available in text typeface designs.

Spine: Main curved stroke of the cap and lowercase "s."

Spur: A small projection from a stroke.

Stem: A vertical or diagonal stroke.

Stress: The direction of thickening in a curved stroke.

Stroke: A single straight or curved line.

Swash Letters: Fancy alternate characters or those with a flourish.

Tail: A short diagonal stroke as in the cap "R," or parts below the baseline as in the lowercase "j" or "y."

Terminal: The end of a stroke not terminated with a serif.

Thin Space: Usually one-fourth to one-fifth of an em.

Uppercase: Capitals; see "Lowercase."

x-Height: Height of lowercase characters not including ascenders and descenders.

Index

This book was typeset at Composition Central and Type Division of Compugraphic Corporation on a Compugraphic EditWriter 7500.

Typefaces used were: Century Old Style for text: Garth Bold Condensed for chapter and running heads. Illustrations were set either on the EditWriter 7500, assembled using dry-transfer sheets from Letraset International Limited, or provided by the T. J. Lyons resource.

Book design by Joan Winer Wilking.